Thank you for considering

MORRIS
PUBLISHING

800-650-7888
www.morrispublishing.com

Book Specifications

Binding: Perfect binding

Cover: Press-ready from client
- Printed in full-color & UV coated
- 10 pt. cover stock

Text: Press-ready from client
- 12.5 pt. Times
- Page numbers centered on bottom of pages
- Page headings:
  Left pages - book title
  Right pages - chapter title
- Black ink on 60 lb. white paper
- 102 pages (including this page)

Special Pages: Title page, copyright page, dedication page, acknowledgement page, table of contents, introduction, bibliography, product listing page, order form, and about the author page.

Our commitment to excellence has made us America's #1 short-run book printer. We are proud to demonstrate the fine quality of our books.

This book is only a printing sample.
Not for Resale.

Becoming
BEHAVIOR

RUTH HARVEY
(FORMERLY RUTH RIEDER)

Becoming Behavior
Copyright © 2005
Ruth Harvey

Cover art by Paul Povolni.

Unless otherwise indicated, all Scripture quotations are taken from the King James Version of the Bible.

ISBN: 978-0-9723182-4-2
First printing: February 2005–500 copies
Second printing: July 2005–1000 copies
Third printing: August 2006–500 copies

FOR INFORMATION CONTACT:
Ruth Harvey
3 Lois Lane
Enfield, CT 06082
505-715-2900

Please visit our web site at
www.positivepowerofholiness.com.
Online ordering is available for all products.

Printed in the USA by
Morris Publishing®
3212 E. Hwy. 30 • Kearney, NE 68847
800-650-7888 • www.morrispublishing.com

Dedicated to the beautiful role models who have impacted my life by their becoming behavior throughout the years, women such as Nona Freeman, Jean Urshan, Alma King, Gwyn Oakes, Joy Haney, Louise Potter, and numerous others who have emulated graceful Christianity on a daily basis. Thank you for the example that has been set before us. My prayer is for my life to have the same powerful impact on those who watch my example and follow in my footsteps.

ACKNOWLEDGEMENTS

Father, Your Spirit and Your Word have been the anchor of my life that has kept me from being swept away by the maelstroms of life. I cling to Your heavenly hand while traversing the dark valleys and sunny vales. Thank You for Your unfailing faithfulness in allowing and enabling me to write yet another treatise. My earnest desire is to know You, to love You, to serve You, and to be like You!

Steven: Daily I thank the Lord for bringing you into my life. Your never ending, unselfish love is the answer to my hungering, heartfelt prayers. God, in His amazing wisdom, set our feet on a pathway of divine destiny so He could bring us together to fulfill His purposes. Thank you for being a godly man of integrity, strength, purity, prayer, and wisdom. You are the man of my dreams, and I love you with all my heart forever and always.

Angel and Miriam: What a daily thrill to see both of you progressing and growing into young ladies of excellence. You have been a light in my darkest night and sunshine in my brightest day. I love you dearly!

Pastor and Sister Burns: Thank you for creating a safe haven for our family to heal and recover from the storms of life.

Bethany Sledge: Thank you for being such an excellent editor who knows how to tweak each nuance of a book and yet retain the flavor of the author's intent and originality— truly a rare gift!

Paul Povolni: It is truly a privilege to work with you. Thank you for communicating the message of this volume through the medium of your superb artwork and design.

TABLE OF CONTENTS

INTRODUCTION

Probably no portion of Scripture encapsulates the biblical role of the woman so perfectly as Titus 2:3-5. In fact, it would seem fitting to call this passage the abbreviated New Testament version of the ladylike qualifications found in Proverbs 31. It reads as follows:

> *"The aged women likewise, that they be in behaviour as becometh holiness, not false accusers, not given to much wine, teachers of good things; that they may teach the young women to be sober, to love their husbands, to love their children, to be discreet, chaste, keepers at home, good, obedient to their own husbands, that the word of God be not blasphemed."*

Using only sixty-three words, the apostle Paul succinctly laid out the perfect pattern for womanhood. If followed, these precepts will enable all ladies to be successful in every area of womanly responsibility. However, to truly glean every valuable nugget contained within this godly advice, it is necessary to examine each nuance and word. To that end, this book lays out each portion of the verses chapter by chapter in order to facilitate this course of diligent study.

My sincere, heartfelt desire is for you, the reader, to realize more fully how important you are in the divine scheme of things. Often we lose sight of how our daily actions generate far-reaching results, either for good or bad, within our families. As we examine ourselves under the microscope of God's Word, let us determine to use our influence for righteousness instead of unrighteousness, for good instead of evil, to replace inappropriate reactions with appropriate responses. May we be holy women of God who demonstrate becoming behavior within our homes, churches, and the world.   ~ Ruth Harvey

Becoming BEHAVIOR

"The aged women likewise, that they be in behaviour as becometh holiness, . . ."

"In the end, it's not the years in your life that count. It's the life in your years." ~ *Abraham Lincoln*

Once again another tidal wave of influence has swept through the country over the past few months. Evidenced by the influx of outrageous red hats coupled with bright purple dresses, this garish combination is actually a statement of humorous rebellion being made by the older generation. Known as the "Red Hat Society," the phenomenon has even taken up residence on the shelves of Wal-Mart and Dillard's, two of our favorite shopping emporia. The latest catalogs also contain many pages of products associated with this popular movement.

A poem penned by Jenny Joseph back in 1961, entitled ***WARNING**, When I Am an Old Woman, I Shall Wear Purple*, has actually been the impetus behind the formation of this society. Voted as Britain's favorite poem in 1996, it advocates rebelling against the parameters of good taste normally followed by refined matrons. Instead of expressing approval for setting an example of well-bred behavior, it venerates a woman who embraces coarse conduct.

This special verse encourages the wearing of mismatched clothing, the misspending of one's pension for liquor and luxuries, and being gluttonous. It also sanctions our elders engaging in unladylike behavior such as pressing alarm bells without cause, intruding into other people's gardens to steal their flowers, and spitting. However, such a mind-set is diametrically opposed to the opening portion of Paul's commentary concerning older women:

> *"The aged women likewise, that they be in behaviour as becometh holiness."*

The apostle was instructing the mature ladies to practice a demeanor which is appropriate or suitable for holy women. Their behavior is supposed to make their holy separation appear attractive to outside observers. In doing a Greek word study of this particular portion of Scripture, it is interesting to note the apostle was actually telling the women their deportment should be so beautiful it would stand out in stark contrast to the ugly attitudes displayed around them. What a tragedy if our testimony becomes nothing more than a travesty because of our unbecoming behavior!

Holiness is so much more than the clothes we wear and the outward obedience to biblical precepts. It also encompasses our daily actions both in public and private settings. Here are some questions to ponder concerning this injunction: What kind of treatment do we mete out to those who wait on us in restaurants? Are we condescending and demanding? Do we seek to "get even" if we did not like their service by leaving an insufficient gratuity, or do we view it as an opportunity to model God's love to them? How do we react when forced to wait in a long line at the store or bank? Do we become easily provoked when driving in heavy traffic and so react with impoliteness?

Are we quick to express our gratitude both verbally and through written notes? When dealing with frustrating situations, do we take out our ire on the salespeople or customer representatives? Would we be able to go back to witness to these people at a later date, or would our earlier actions negate that possibility?

The value of these thought-provoking questions was brought home to me on a very personal level during two separate incidents. The first took place on a Sunday evening when a large group from our church descended upon a local eating establishment. During the course of the night, our waiter was somewhat absent-minded and, consequently, several of the orders were mixed up. However, I was so thankful that everyone took it in stride and acted very Christlike, even leaving the young man quite a sizable tip. When we exited the restaurant, our waiter thanked us profusely for our patience with his errors and also for giving him a generous gratuity in spite of the mix-up with our orders. As our group continued visiting in the parking lot, this same young man got off work and called out as he walked by, "I'm out of here." Prompted by the Lord, I made my way to him and invited him to visit our church. After I told him about our location and service times, he earnestly thanked me for the invitation and indicated his interest in checking out our church. While walking to my car, I realized anew how our actions can have far-reaching eternal consequences. If we had treated our waiter with impatient insolence, would my invitation have been welcomed or disdained? Indeed, he had already "checked out" our church without ever walking through its doors.

The other incident took place at a local Walgreen's when I was waiting in line at the checkout. As the man in front of me began placing his items on the counter, not only did he move slowly, but he also became argumentative with the clerk about a particular price of an item. Feeling that old surge of impatience rise within me, I had an immediate desire to react in a negative manner. Thankfully, the Lord dealt with me, and I felt the responsibility of being an ambassador for Jesus Christ settle upon my shoulders. Observing the man in question more closely, I realized he was injured and seemed to be in a great deal of pain. After further inquiry, he told me how his recent back surgery had gone awry. My heart was smitten because I had almost reacted out of my impatience instead of responding to his need. Still, God was gracious and checked me before I ruined a golden opportunity to model becoming behavior in a frustrating circumstance. In the end, this man, whose name was Todd, allowed me to pray for him. After he expressed his gratitude for my prayers, I extended an invitation to visit our church. As Todd walked painfully out the door, I breathed a heartfelt and sincere prayer that somewhere, someday he would walk through the doors of the church and find eternal relief from the suffering of sin. It makes me shudder to think of how my testimony could have suffered a severe setback if the Holy Ghost had not quickened a more compassionate response within my heart. Lord, may we be more sensitive and gracious to the hurting multitudes that surround us!

On a more personal note, how do we treat our family on a daily basis? Oftentimes those closest to us are the unfortunate recipients of our pent-up rage. Do our homes become battlegrounds or places of safe sanctuary? Progressing in our study throughout the pages of this book, we will take an in-depth look at the becoming behavior which should accompany our holiness. If our uncut hair is not coupled with a spirit of submission, it will not be nearly as attractive. Modest apparel is much more flattering if paired with a gracious, respectful attitude. An unpainted face should be wreathed in smiles in order to maximize its beauty. Lamentably, our outward manifestation of holiness may be viewed through others' jaundiced perceptions if it is tainted by ugly actions and attitudes spewed from the corrupt inner fountain of our hearts.

In I Peter 2:11-16, the apostle adjured:

> *"Dearly beloved, I beseech you as strangers and pilgrims, abstain from fleshly lusts, which war against the soul;* **having your conversation honest among the Gentiles: that, whereas they speak against you as evildoers, they may by your good works, which they shall behold, glorify God in the day of visitation.** *Submit yourselves to every ordinance of man for the Lord's sake: whether it be to the king, as supreme; or unto governors, as unto them that are sent by him for the punishment of evildoers, and for the praise of them that do well. For so is the will of God,* **that with well doing ye may put to silence the ignorance of foolish men:** *as free, and not using your liberty for a cloke of maliciousness, but as the servants of God."*

Our becoming behavior should make God's kingdom look good!

For the past several weeks, the words of an old song have been resounding in my heart and spirit:

To Be Like Him

From Bethl'hem's manger came forth a Stranger,
On earth I long to be like Him;
My faithful Savior, how rich His favor!
On earth I long to be like Him.

Serene and holy, obedient, lowly
On earth I long to be like Him;
By grace forgiven, an heir of heaven,
On earth I long to be like Him.

To be like Jesus,
To be like Jesus,
On earth I long to be like Him;
All thru life's journey from earth to glory
I only ask to be like Him.[1]

And that, my friend, is the pure, delightful sum and substance of Becoming Behavior—to be like our Savior!

Chapter One Footnote:

1. "To Be Like Him," composed by L. R. Ooton.

Troublemakers
OR PEACEMAKERS

". . . not false accusers, . . ."

"It is not within everyone's power to be beautiful, but all of us can make sure that the words that come out of our mouths are."
~ Jewish proverb

A Greek philosopher asked his servant to provide the best dish possible. The servant prepared a dish of tongue, saying, "It is the best of all dishes, because with it we may bless and communicate happiness, dispel sorrow, remove despair, cheer the fainthearted, inspire the discouraged, and say a hundred other things to uplift mankind." Later the philosopher asked his servant to provide the worst dish of which he could think. A dish of tongue appeared on the table. The servant said, "It is the worst, because with it we may curse and break human hearts; destroy reputations; promote discord and strife; set families, communities, and nations at war with each other." He was a wise servant.[1]

Ah, the power of the tongue! Throughout His Word, God Himself recognized and reiterated many times the infiltrating force of our speech. This is reflected in numerous passages of Scripture but especially so in James, chapter 3. That the Holy Spirit compelled the holy writers of old to focus so forcefully on a particular subject is a sure indication of its extreme eternal importance. Let us examine more closely what the apostle James communicated concerning the destructive and constructive capability of this smallest member in our body:

"My brethren, be not many masters, knowing that we shall receive the greater condemnation. For in many things we offend all. If any man offend not in word, the same is a perfect man, and able also to bridle the whole body. Behold, we put bits in the horses' mouths, that they may obey us; and we turn about their whole body. Behold also the ships, which though they be so great, and are driven of fierce winds, yet are they turned about with a very small helm, whithersoever the governor listeth. Even so the tongue is a little member, and boasteth great things. Behold, how great a matter a little fire kindleth! And the tongue is a fire, a world of iniquity: so is the tongue among our members, that it defileth the whole body, and setteth on fire the course of nature; and it is set on fire of hell. For every kind of beasts, and of birds, and of serpents, and of things in the sea, is tamed, and hath been tamed of mankind: but the tongue can no man tame; it is an unruly evil, full of deadly poison. Therewith bless we God, even the Father; and therewith curse we men, which are made after the similitude of God. Out of the same mouth proceedeth blessing and cursing. My brethren, these things ought not so to be. Doth a fountain send forth at the same place sweet water and bitter? Can the fig tree,

my brethren, bear olive berries? either a vine,
figs? so can no fountain both yield salt water
and fresh."

First of all, James cautioned against desiring a place of leadership, because so much more is required of those in a prominent position, especially when it comes to the matter of ruling one's speech. As is so often the case, people have a long tongue and a short fuse. In reality, if we ever hope to become effective in our influence, it is imperative to have a short tongue coupled with a long fuse. As former President Calvin Coolidge wisely stated, "I've never been hurt by anything I didn't say." Unfortunately, it is so much easier and seemingly more enjoyable to yield to the destructive power of ungoverned communication. Nevertheless, in the end we become our own worst enemy and are hurt the most by such actions. "People who have sharp tongues soon cut their own throats." The following statement is very sagacious advice: "The real art of conversation is not only to say the right thing in the right place but also to leave unsaid the wrong thing at the tempting moment."

The ability to govern one's tongue is an indicator of complete self-control in every other area of life. As the wise man Solomon averred so long ago:

> *"He that hath knowledge spareth his words: and*
> *a man of understanding is of an excellent spirit.*
> *Even a fool, when he holdeth his peace, is*
> *counted wise: and he that shutteth his lips is*
> *esteemed a man of understanding."* [2]

Recently a wise pastor's wife told me that she refuses to pass along destructive information to her husband that could cloud his ability to properly oversee the flock of God for which he is responsible. This lady was definitely engaging in becoming behavior. Instead of fomenting trouble and filling his mind with negative thoughts, she has learned to hold her peace so the Lord can give clear, untainted direction to her pastor husband. It would behoove all ladies to embrace and prudently practice the same kind of comely conduct.

Continuing in our examination of his passage, James spoke of the human ability to control a huge horse with a small bit and to steer a sizable ship with a small helm. Likewise, the destined course of our lives will be directly influenced by whether we can control our tiny tongue which I sometimes call "the little red devil behind the pearly white gates." It is astounding what havoc can be wrought by the littlest part of our body. It has been wisely observed that "a tongue three inches long can ruin a man six feet tall."

Sadly, we can engage in high praises during an anointed church service, only to exit the sacred precincts and get caught up in passing along the latest gossip to our buddies at the local eatery. One moment we can be praising God, and in the next breath it is possible to mutilate someone's reputation beyond repair. The same mouth should not spew out blessing and cursing. This sort of behavior does not enhance our Christianity but rather detracts from it.

Lamentably, "nothing is easier than faultfinding; no talent, no self-denial, no brains, no character are required to set up in the grumbling business."

Words Like Arrows

How like an arrow is a word
At random often speeding

To find a target never meant
And set some heart a-bleeding.
Oh, pray that Heaven may seal the lips
Ere unkind words are spoken;
For Heaven itself cannot recall,
When once the seal is broken.
~ Excerpted from
The Evangelist and Bible Teacher

The preceding poem brings to mind a prudent prayer which simply says, "Lord, put Your arm around my shoulder and Your hand over my mouth." Likewise, in Psalm 141:3, David entreated the Lord:

"Set a watch, O LORD, before my mouth; keep
the door of my lips."

The climate control of our homes and lives is directly affected by the thermostat of our words. What sort of conversation is proceeding out of our mouths on a daily basis? Is it laudatory and loving or harsh and hateful?

A Harsh Word

One day a harsh word, harshly said,
Upon an evil journey sped,
And like a sharp and cruel dart,
It pierced a fond and loving heart.

It turned a friend into a foe
And everywhere brought pain and woe.
A kind word followed it one day,
Sped swiftly on its blessed way.

It healed the wound and soothed the pain,
And friends of old were friends again.
It made the hate and anger cease,
And everywhere brought joy and peace.

And yet the harsh word left a trace
The kind word could not efface,
And though the heart its love regained
It left a scar that long remained.

Friends can forgive but not forget,
Nor lose the sense of keen regret.
Oh, if we would but learn to know
How swift and sure our words can go.

How we would weigh with utmost care
Each thought before it reached the air—
And only speak the words that move
Like white-winged messengers of love.[3]

An old saying declares, "Sticks and stones may break my bones, but words can never hurt me." In reality, nothing could be further from the truth. Wounding words can create ongoing emotional fallout, which is very difficult to overcome. Victims of emotional and verbal abuse can testify of the long-term damage inflicted by destructive verbiage. Long after physical injuries heal, the inner trauma of damaging discord continues to exert its influence in the life of the victim.

In Proverbs 18:21, Solomon illustrated the fruit-bearing nature of the spoken word:

"Death and life are in the power of the tongue:
and they that love it shall eat the fruit thereof."

Our speech will reproduce either life-giving love or deadly damage, and in the end we will be forced to partake of this produce. Wouldn't it be much more palatable to eat the product of sweetly seasoned speech?

> *"Let your speech be always with grace, seasoned with salt, that ye may know how ye ought to answer every man."*[4]

Death or Life in Words

> *A careless word may kindle strife,*
> *A cruel word may wreck a life;*
> *A bitter word may hate instill,*
> *A brutal word may smite and kill;*
> *A gracious word may smooth the way,*
> *A joyous word may light this day;*
> *A timely word may lessen stress,*
> *A loving word may heal and bless.*[5]

Be careful with your words, for you may have to eat them someday. "Lord, help me watch the words I say and keep them few and sweet. For I don't know from day to day which ones I'll have to eat!"

Given women's penchant for engaging in continual conversation, perhaps no other area of our lives is so pertinent to producing Becoming Behavior. Have you ever observed a woman who is outwardly attractive until she opens her mouth and utters uncouth comments? Our speech has the power to enhance our attractiveness or rather quickly destroy it. Following in this same vein of thought, a rather humorous exchange was made between John Wesley and an unnamed woman. She said, "My talent is to speak my mind." To which Wesley answered, "I am sure, Sister, that God wouldn't mind if you buried **THAT** talent!" An unknown philosopher once said, "Mind what you say, or you might say whatever comes to mind."

As was mentioned earlier, the Bible is replete with admonitions about the government of the gift of gab. For the sake of enhancing our study, a condensed list of admonitions from the Book of Proverbs concerning the taming of the tongue is listed below:

> *"Put away from thee a froward mouth, and per-verse lips put far from thee" (Proverbs 4:24).*

> *"In the multitude of words there wanteth not sin: but he that refraineth his lips is wise. The tongue of the just is as choice silver: the heart of the wicked is little worth. The lips of the righteous feed many: but fools die for want of wisdom" (Proverbs 10:19-21).*

> *"The mouth of the just bringeth forth wisdom: but the froward tongue shall be cut out. The lips of the righteous know what is acceptable: but the mouth of the wicked speaketh forwardness" (Proverbs 10:31-32).*

> *"The wicked is snared by the transgression of his lips: but the just shall come out of trouble" (Proverbs 12:13).*

> *"He that speaketh truth sheweth forth righteous-ness: but a false witness deceit. There is that speaketh like the piercings of a sword: but the tongue of the wise is health. The lip of truth*

shall be established for ever: but a lying tongue is but for a moment" (Proverbs 12:17-19).

"Lying lips are an abomination to the LORD: but they that deal truly are his delight" (Proverbs 12:22).

"A man shall eat good by the fruit of his mouth: but the soul of the transgressors shall eat violence. He that keepeth his mouth keepeth his life: but he that openeth wide his lips shall have destruction" (Proverbs 13:2-3).

"In the mouth of the foolish is a rod of pride: but the lips of the wise shall preserve them" (Proverbs 14:3).

"A soft answer turneth away wrath: but grievous words stir up anger. The tongue of the wise useth knowledge aright: but the mouth of fools poureth out foolishness" (Proverbs 15:1-2).

"A wholesome tongue is a tree of life: but perverseness therein is a breach in the spirit" (Proverbs 15:4).

"The lips of the wise disperse knowledge: but the heart of the foolish doeth not so" (Proverbs 15:7).

"A man hath joy by the answer of his mouth: and a word spoken in due season, how good is it!" (Proverbs 15:23).

"The heart of the righteous studieth to answer: but the mouth of the wicked poureth out evil things" (Proverbs 15:28).

"Righteous lips are the delight of kings; and they love him that speaketh right" (Proverbs 16:13).

"The wise in heart shall be called prudent: and the sweetness of the lips increaseth learning" (Proverbs 16:21).

"The heart of the wise teacheth his mouth, and addeth learning to his lips. Pleasant words are as an honeycomb, sweet to the soul, and health to the bones" (Proverbs 16:23-24).

"An ungodly man diggeth up evil: and in his lips there is as a burning fire. A froward man soweth strife: and a whisperer separateth chief friends" (Proverbs 16:27-28).

"Excellent speech becometh not a fool: much less do lying lips a prince" (Proverbs 17:7).

"He that hath a froward heart findeth no good: and he that hath a perverse tongue falleth into mischief" (Proverbs 17:20).

"The words of a man's mouth are as deep waters, and the wellspring of wisdom as a flowing brook" (Proverbs 18:4).

"A fool's lips enter into contention, and his mouth calleth for strokes. A fool's mouth is his destruction, and his lips are the snare of his soul. The words of a talebearer are as wounds, and they go down into the innermost parts of the belly" (Proverbs 18:6-8).

"He that answereth a matter before he heareth it, it is folly and shame unto him" (Proverbs 18:13).

"There is gold, and a multitude of rubies: but the lips of knowledge are a precious jewel" (Proverbs 20:15).

"He that goeth about as a talebearer revealeth secrets: therefore meddle not with him that flattereth with his lips" (Proverbs 20:19).

"He that loveth pureness of heart, for the grace of his lips the king shall be his friend" (Proverbs 22:11).

"My son, if thine heart be wise, my heart shall rejoice, even mine. Yea, my reins shall rejoice, when thy lips speak right things" (Proverbs 23:15-16).

"Every man shall kiss his lips that giveth a right answer" (Proverbs 24:26).

"A word fitly spoken is like apples of gold in pictures of silver" (Proverbs 25:11).

"The words of a talebearer are as wounds, and they go down into the innermost parts of the belly. Burning lips and a wicked heart are like a potsherd covered with silver dross. He that hateth dissembleth with his lips, and layeth up deceit within him; when he speaketh fair, believe him not: for there are seven abominations in his heart. Whose hatred is covered by deceit, his wickedness shall be shewed before the whole congregation" (Proverbs 26:22-26).

"A lying tongue hateth those that are afflicted by it; and a flattering mouth worketh ruin" (Proverbs 26:28).

As we can see from the preceding verses, every aspect of our lives is affected by what comes out of our mouths. The quality of our lives and relationships is either enhanced or eroded by the power of our words. In one fell swoop, we can utterly demolish others with a wrecking ball called the tongue. Depending on how we wield this powerful tool of communication, it becomes either a weapon of war or a producer of peace. Our words can build up or tear down, edify or destroy, create life or introduce death. All with the slip of the tongue or the taming of it.

The literal Greek word for *false accusers* is **diabolos**, meaning "satan, devil, slanderer." Paul admonished the women not to become accusatory like satan, who is identified as "the accuser of our brethren" in Revelation 12:10. This verse further states that it is his diabolical practice to accuse us before our God day and night. Because of a woman's fertile imagination, how easy it often becomes to get caught up in the vicious cycle of gossip, making false accusations and believing imaginary scenarios which do not even exist. This sort of unbecoming behavior can wreak havoc in a home, a church, a marriage, a life. II Corinthians 10:5 tells us how to deal with this sort of behavior:

> *"Casting down imaginations, and every high thing that exalteth itself against the knowledge of God, and bringing into captivity every thought to the obedience of Christ."*

Further instruction is found in James 1:19-20:

> *"Wherefore, my beloved brethren, let every man be swift to hear, slow to speak, slow to wrath: for the wrath of man worketh not the righteousness of God."*

Cotton Mather made the following wise observation concerning this biblical injunction, "Men are born with two eyes but with one tongue, that they may see twice as much as they say." While penning these precepts, another little judicious, poetic proverb echoes in my mind:

> *A wise old owl sat in an oak*
> *The more he saw, the less he spoke*
> *The less he spoke, the more he heard*
> *Why can't we be more like that wise old bird?*

A person who is unable to control his or her communication will suffer in every other area of life. Solomon wisely warned us in Proverbs 29:20:

> *"Seest thou a man that is hasty in his words? there is more hope of a fool than of him."*

31

As W. B. Knight so wisely stated, "Our temper is one of the few things that improves the longer we keep it." Again, another unknown wise sage humorously said, "Nothing will cook your goose quicker than a red hot temper."

In the final portion of James 3, the apostle contrasted earthly and heavenly wisdom:

> *"Who is a wise man and endued with knowledge among you? let him shew out of a good conversation his works with meekness of wisdom. But if ye have bitter envying and strife in your hearts, glory not, and lie not against the truth. This wisdom descendeth not from above, but is earthly, sensual, devilish. For where envying and strife is, there is confusion and every evil work. But the wisdom that is from above is first pure, then peaceable, gentle, and easy to be intreated, full of mercy and good fruits, without partiality, and without hypocrisy. And the fruit of righteousness is sown in peace of them that make peace."*

What an incredible divinely inspired juxtaposition of the two kinds of wisdom! One creates strife, the other produces peace. We can live in a state of confusion or engender graceful gentility. It all depends on the mastery of our littlest member. As this chapter comes to conclusion, the subsequent rhyme offers some universally discriminating advice:

The Tongue

*"The boneless tongue, so small and weak,
Can crush and kill," declares the Greek.*

"The tongue destroys the greater horde,"
The Turk asserts, "than does the sword."
The Persian proverb wisely saith,
"A lengthy tongue—an early death!"
Or sometimes takes this form instead,
"Don't let your tongue cut off your head."
"The tongue can speak a word whose speed,"
Say the Chinese, "outstrips the steeds."
The Arab sages said in part,
"The tongue's great storehouse is the heart."
From Hebrew was the maxim sprung,
"Thy feet should slip, ne'er let the tongue."
The sacred writer crowns the whole,
"Who keeps his tongue doth keep his soul."[6]

Please, for the sake of those you love, think before you speak. Instead of being troublemakers, let us become peacemakers, for then we shall be called the children of God. Now that is definitely divinely becoming behavior!

Chapter Two Footnotes:

1. Walter B. Knight, *Knight's Master Book of New Illustrations* (Wm. B. Eerdmans Publishing Company, 1956), p. 691.
2. Proverbs 17:27-28.
3. Knight, *Illustrations*, p. 690.
4. Colossians 4:6.
5. Knight, *Illustrations*, p. 693.
6. Knight, *Illustrations*, p. 692.

INFLUENCES

". . . not given to much wine, . . ."

"In today's complex and fast-moving world, what we need even more than foresight or hindsight is insight."　　　*~ Unknown*

In Matthew 24:38-39, Jesus identified out-of-control appetites as a sign of the last days:

> *"For as in the days that were before the flood they were eating and drinking, marrying and giving in marriage, until the day that Noe entered into the ark, and knew not until the flood came, and took them all away; so shall also the coming of the Son of man be."*

Again in Luke 17:26-30, He alluded to the domination of desires during the end times:

> *"And as it was in the days of Noe, so shall it be also in the days of the Son of man. They did eat, they drank, they married wives, they were given in marriage, until the day that Noe entered into the ark, and the flood came, and destroyed them all. Likewise also as it was in the days of*

Lot; they did eat, they drank, they bought, they sold, they planted, they builded; but the same day that Lot went out of Sodom it rained fire and brimstone from heaven, and destroyed them all. Even thus shall it be in the day when the Son of man is revealed."

One of the more infamous cultural maxims selfishly declares, "If it feels good, do it!" The rampant hedonism of our society lends license to capriciously engage in satisfying one's lust. Drinking, carousing, revelry, illicit affairs, gluttonous gorging, and over-spending are just some of the out-of-control symptoms which prevail throughout the land. In this modern day, being held captive in the bonds of an addiction is a common thread which runs throughout many lives. Continually driven by illicit appetites, more and more people are indulging their insatiable desire for drink and drugs. Becoming intoxicated during "happy hours" is now the focal point of many. An entire restaurant chain called T.G.I.Friday's or "Thank God It's Friday" embodies the intoxicating influences which permeate our culture.

However, this sort of mind-set is not biblically based. Throughout God's Word we are commanded to control our urges, especially so in this particular portion of our study. Paul averred that godly women should not be given to much wine. Given the fact that we espouse abstinence from intoxicating beverages, what deeper insight can be gleaned from his injunction? As stated in the previous paragraph, alcohol is an intoxicating substance. What exactly does it mean to become intoxicated? According to *Webster's Dictionary*, it is defined as "to induce, esp. with ingested alcohol, effects ranging from exhilaration to stupefaction; to stimulate or excite." Interestingly enough, the word from which *intoxicate* originates literally means "to put poison in." So to become intoxicated actually means to partake of a substance which brings you under its addictive power and produces harmful side effects that can poison your life. As is most often the case, the reason people give themselves unreservedly to an alcoholic addiction is because of deeper problematic issues which lie buried beneath the surface of their lives. Conditions such as mental, verbal, physical, or sexual abuse, low self esteem, depression, or lack of spiritual direction are just a few of the factors which can influence this sort of behavioral pattern. Sadly, the ingesting of intoxicating substances only serves to exacerbate one's problems by producing a vicious cycle of drinking until giddy or stupefied, only to awaken to the horrendous side effects of a hangover. One drink continues to call for another as the deadly pattern habitually repeats itself until lives are destroyed one swallow at a time.

Understandably, our consecrated Christian lifestyle prohibits becoming involved in this sort of addictive conduct. Nevertheless, it is so vital for us to face the fact that many in our churches may be dealing with unresolved issues of abuse and depression, which in turn can inhibit spiritual growth. When these underlying problems are not dealt with properly through the healing power of the Word, a daily prayer life, fasting, and faithfulness to God, they can cause abnormal addictive behavioral patterns.

There are many other ways an intoxicating influence can be introduced into a life, and the enemy of our soul would love nothing more than to get us hung up in a cycle of binging behavior. It is not unusual for women and even men to drown their inner pain in the destructive cycle of overeating, overspending, reading endless mind-numbing novels that create an unrealistic fantasy world, or even listening to worldly music.

Understandably, it is not wrong to eat. We have to eat to

live; however, many people begin living to eat until their appetites are out of control. Then the vicious cycle of self-hate sets in when looking in the mirror at bloated bodies and ill-fitting clothing. Oftentimes women begin to let themselves go and no longer practice good grooming habits, which only serves to make them feel worse and can create a variety of hostile responses within the home and marriage relationships. Oftentimes self-loathing is the underlying cause of angry outbursts. An unattractive outward appearance coupled with inner ugliness may actually create a very harmful scenario of cyclical hostility, which can batter even the strongest relationships. When talking with people who suffer in this area of their lives, I have often found they are using food as a comfort mechanism in order to stuff down the deeper symptoms of inward wounds. Without conscious thought, the gluttonous process is repeated as many stuff their faces with food even when hunger is not present. Unfortunately, instead of aiding in the process of inner healing, this sort of conduct only compounds the problem.

Another addictive behavior can be overspending. Again, an occasional shopping trip to the mall is not wrong and money must be spent for life's necessities. Still, some women get caught up in believing another new outfit or household item will assuage their inner emptiness. Let me confess to you, the reader, that at one point in my life, I got caught up in this sort of response. Time after time, I would find myself at the store, buying an exorbitant amount of clothing and accessories on credit. Then I would hide it in my closet to wear a little at a time so my overspending would not be so obvious to my spouse. Unfortunately, it came time to pay the piper when the huge credit card bills started coming in the mail. Then panic over our beleaguered finances set in, which only compounded my mental stress. Again it was a vicious, intoxicating influence that could not resolve my inner issues. By earnestly seeking for God's help through consistent daily prayer and study, I managed to extricate myself from this destructive and costly cycle. Only a deep, personal relationship with Jesus could satisfy the longings of my soul. After a while a new outfit becomes dated and loses its appeal or is destroyed by rips or stains, but being in close communion with God will produce an age-less fulfillment which never goes out of style. In fact, it only becomes more beautiful with age and sweeter as the years go by.

> *Sweeter as the years go by,*
> *Sweeter as the years go by;*
> *Richer, fuller, deeper,*
> *Jesus' love is sweeter,*
> *Sweeter as the years go by.*[1]

Other addictive influences can be found in the form of ingesting harmful reading materials or listening to ungodly music. These avenues of entrance into our thought processes may manufacture unreal expectations in personal relationships and can also introduce a worldly mind-set. Sometimes women who are not happy at home seek to drown their dissatisfaction by filling their minds with fictitious fantasy. Again, this does not alleviate the problem but only makes them more unhappy with their present circumstances. Instead of appreciating God's daily blessings and looking for ways in which to improve themselves, they get caught up in chasing an ethereal, nonexistent ideal. All the while, their complaint of discontentment may cause them to denigrate their husbands and place unreasonable demands upon them which can tear down a godly union.

So how can these unresolved issues be dealt with effectively? First of all, it is important to identify the source of the problem instead of covering it with food, finances, or fantasies. Once the taproot of trouble is unearthed, it can be uprooted through the power of reading and memorizing God's Word. Every antidote for our addictions can be found in the pages of Holy Writ. Releasing divine energy, the Word can enable us to exercise control over our flesh. Furthermore, it reveals the depth of God's true and unconditional love. Like a healing balm, it will restore soundness to the mind as God's perspective replaces the faulty perceptions of the carnal mind-set. Instead of popping pills such as Valium or Prozac, why not fill up on a daily prescription of memorized biblical passages? It is amazing how the Scriptures will renew hope, reestablish faith, reinstate love, and restore godliness with contentment.

Another component of complete inner deliverance is found in daily communion with your Creator. As the songwriter said so beautifully, "In the presence of Jehovah, troubles vanish; hearts are mended in the presence of the King." Fullness of joy will never be found in another plate of food, a new outfit, an updated decorating scheme, or in the pages of the latest steamy novel. In Psalm 16:11, the psalmist David identified the only true source of lasting joy:

> *"Thou wilt shew me the path of life: in thy presence is fulness of joy; at thy right hand there are pleasures for evermore."*

Practicing the presence of God will produce inner tranquility.

A third factor in overcoming intoxicating influences is to stop being self-focused and self-absorbed. As the old adage declares, "The smallest package in the world is the person wrapped up in himself." If you will get outside yourself and begin to minister to the needs of others, it will amaze you how quickly your focus will change to one of overcoming exultation. Teach a home Bible study, visit the sick, volunteer to clean the church, get involved in ministry, and suddenly as you give of yourself, life circumstances will no longer have the power to control you.

As I was going through the incredible agony of betrayal and divorce, my district superintendent, Bro. Terry Pugh, gave me some of the wisest advice. He instructed me to keep all my speaking engagements, to attend every conference, and to stay totally involved in the work of the Lord. This, of course, forced me to be accountable for my time by preparing messages that would be of help to others. It also necessitated the spiritual maintenance of my personal walk with God so I could be prepared to minister effectively. Moreover, the maintaining of my responsibilities kept me occupied so I didn't have time to degenerate into hopeless depression. Another plus was the loving, supportive fellowship that was extended to me as I stayed close to the body of Christ.

At times it was so difficult to give out when it seemed I was nothing but an empty shell. Nevertheless, every time I reached beyond my hurt and gave of myself to others, it enabled me to endure the emotional trauma which had rocked my world. To be quite honest, many were the times I would weep profusely in my motel room just prior to a meeting, wondering how in the world it would be possible to reach out to others when I was hurting so bad. Yet every time I walked to the pulpit, God met me and His strength was made perfect in my profound weakness. Yes, there were days I did not want to live; times when it was almost impossible to keep putting one foot in front of the other. But the ability to overcome was not found in external avenues of escape such as eating, shopping, reading novels, or taking medication. It was found in the pages of God's Word.

Over and over I would desperately quote Psalm 118:17:

> *"I shall not die, but live, and declare the works
> of the LORD."*

Today my life is a living testimony of the creative, keeping power of the Word. It sustained me, preserved my strength, and protected my mind. Additionally, the continual spiritual connection found in the prayer closet enabled me to tap into God's divine, sustaining power as He would wrap His gentle arms around me and hold me close. From my own personal experience, I found the components of prayer, the Word, and helping others to be key in finding my own private place of inner healing. Likewise, you will find, as you allow these effectual spiritual tools to work in your own hurtful circumstances, they will enable you to overcome every obstacle. Instead of allowing the past to master you, through the power of God, you can become the master of your past pain. One of the most remarkable things that will transpire through your triumphant transformation is that when God turns your tragedy into triumph, your pain into peace, and your hurt into helping others, never again will the old intoxicating influences hold you captive.

> *"If the Son therefore shall make you free, ye
> shall be free indeed."*[2]

Chapter Three Footnotes:

1. Words and music by Lelia N. Morris, copyright 1912.
2. John 8:36.

Wise Women
TEACHERS

"... teachers of good things; that they may teach the young women to be sober, ..."

"I tell you and you forget. I show you and you remember. I involve you and you understand."   ~ Eric Butterworth

From the dawn of Creation, the woman immediately stepped into the role of instructing others. The first classroom teaching experience took place right in the Garden of Eden. After taking the first bite of the forbidden fruit, Eve proceeded to offer it to Adam. Following her example of disobedience, the man also chose to act contrary to God's laws. Thus, Eve taught Adam to sin both by example and invitation.

Continuing in the footsteps of his recalcitrant parents, Cain, their eldest son, offered an improper sacrifice to God. Even when confronted by the Almighty concerning the impropriety of his offering, Cain refused to repent. His insurgency escalated even further when the sacrifice of his brother Abel was accepted by God. This caused Cain to be filled with jealousy. Then driven by his disobedient, jealous rage, he murdered Abel and subsequently refused to take responsibility for the crime. His defiant disdain for God's laws resulted in his expulsion from the Almighty's presence.

Running pell-mell down the same pathway of rebellion, humankind continues to follow in the footsteps of their original parents even to this present day. If this trend is ever to be reversed, strong action must be taken on a daily basis within our homes. Continuing in our exploration of Paul's writings in Titus 2:3-5, the apostle revealed the best plan of action for women to take in this important area. It is imperative for them to become *"teachers of good things."* Furthermore, they are instructed to teach the young women to be sober, which actually means to be wise. What this world needs more of is **wise women teachers**.

Today's world has given a false set of values to women and girls. Instead of preparing the female gender to function appropriately in their God-ordained roles as wives and mothers, the feminist movement decries all that is good and right according to God's Word. Replacing the normal nurturing ways of the fairer sex, the feminist propaganda has instilled a destructive self-centeredness within women. Now they are brainwashed into believing it is more constructive if their focus is on a career rather than being a care-giver and all at the expense of the solvency of the family unit. Even the church is not immune to this voice. Harried women who were never meant to carry the working load of the business world find themselves on the merry-go-round of super achievement. However, it is so important to understand there are simply not enough hours in a day or enough energy in a woman's body to be Super Businesswoman, Super Mom, Super Wife, and Super Christian 24/7. In the end, this race for success takes a very injurious toll on the female body and psyche. Could this be why there are more angry and out-of-control women than ever before?

The solution is simple—we must return to the basics of instilling in each generation the wisdom of God's plan for the woman. In I Timothy 2:15, Paul laid out some vital areas in which women can excel on a daily basis:

"Notwithstanding she shall be saved in child-bearing, if they continue in faith and charity and holiness with sobriety."

You may be asking how childbearing could be a means of salvation. Simply put, if a wise mother will instill the proper value system within her children, the stage is set for the cycle of salvation to be put in motion within her family from generation to generation. Oh, the power of wise woman teachers! Think of what our world could become if we began to practice these principles one woman at a time, one family at a time, one church at a time. . . The possibilities are powerful. We could literally change our world and undo the destructive instruction of Eve, the first woman teacher.

Let us focus on the three vital areas referred to in I Timothy 2:15. The first is identified as "faith." According to *Strong's Exhaustive Concordance*, this is the Greek word **pistis**, which is pronounced *pis'-tis*. It means to have a moral conviction of the truthfulness of God and His Word, to be persuaded about the plan of salvation, and to have an assurance of your belief system. How many are able to properly explain the essential components of truth to their children? If our children question our biblical belief system, will we be able to tell them why they must obey these precepts? It is imperative that we are able to explain the whys and wherefores of repentance, water baptism in Jesus' name, the infilling of the Holy Ghost, and the necessity of practicing obedience to the laws of God. Now, more than ever, a call is being issued for "wise women teachers" to step up and fulfill their spiritual obligation to pass along these precious precepts to their posterity!

The next area of importance is "charity." This is probably one of the most key ingredients in successful Christianity. Ralph Waldo Emerson stated, "Love is the essence of God." I Corinthians 13:13 identifies charity as the greatest attribute of all. In John 13:35, Jesus established it as the premier mark of discipleship. Furthermore, the book of I John classifies this particular quality as a prerequisite for eternal salvation.

"He that saith he is in the light, and hateth his brother, is in darkness even until now. He that loveth his brother abideth in the light, and there is none occasion of stumbling in him. But he that hateth his brother is in darkness, and walketh in darkness, and knoweth not whither he goeth, because that darkness hath blinded his eyes" (I John 2:9-11).

"We know that we have passed from death unto life, because we love the brethren. He that loveth not his brother abideth in death. Whosoever hateth his brother is a murderer: and ye know that no murderer hath eternal life abiding in him. Hereby perceive we the love of God, because he laid down his life for us: and we ought to lay down our lives for the brethren. But whoso hath this world's good, and seeth his brother have need, and shutteth up his bowels of compassion from him, how dwelleth the love of God in him? My little children, let us not love in word, neither in tongue; but in deed and in truth" (I John 3:14-18).

"Beloved, let us love one another: for love is of God; and every one that loveth is born of God, and knoweth God. He that loveth not knoweth not God; for God is love" (I John 4:7-8).

"And we have known and believed the love that God hath to us. God is love; and he that dwelleth in love dwelleth in God, and God in him. Herein is our love made perfect, that we may have boldness in the day of judgment: because as he is, so are we in this world. There is no fear in love; but perfect love casteth out fear: because fear hath torment. He that feareth is not made perfect in love. We love him, because he first loved us. If a man say, I love God, and hateth his brother, he is a liar: for he that loveth not his brother whom he hath seen, how can he love God whom he hath not seen? And this commandment have we from him, That he who loveth God love his brother also" (I John 4:16-21).

"Whosoever believeth that Jesus is the Christ is born of God: and every one that loveth him that begat loveth him also that is begotten of him. By this we know that we love the children of God, when we love God, and keep his commandments" (I John 5:1-2).

As can be ascertained from reading these powerful passages of Scripture from I John, love for God and for one another is not an option. It is a requirement if we hope to make heaven our home. Our churches, marriages, and homes must become fountains which disperse the warmth of God's love on a continual basis. Henry Ward Beecher aptly summed up love's potency, "Love is the river of life in this world. Not until you have gone through the rocky gorges, and not lost the stream; not until you have gone through the meadow, and the stream has widened and deepened . . . not until you have come to the unfathomable ocean, and poured your treasures into its depths—not until then can you know what love is." Love will cause us to move beyond ourselves into a realm of unselfish giving where others' needs come before the achieving of our own self-motivated desires. "Love seeks one thing only: the good of the one loved. It leaves all the other secondary effects to take care of themselves. Love, therefore, is its own reward" (Thomas Merton).

When charity becomes the supreme governor of our actions, responses, and attitudes, the blessings of God will be released upon our lives in great measure. The more we love, the more we will be loved. "Love is not merely a contributor . . . to meaningful life. In its own way it may underlie all other forms of meaning" (Irving Singer). The love of God will cause us to treat one another in a more Christlike way, thereby introducing a greater measure of peace and harmony in our lives, our homes, our marriages, and our churches.

Solomon, the wise sage, gave us some wonderful advice in Proverbs 10:12 and 17:9 concerning the power of love:

> *"Hatred stirreth up strifes: but love covereth all sins. . . . He that covereth a transgression seeketh love; but he that repeateth a matter separateth very friends."*

Strife, contention, and arguments will cease if loving ways are practiced on a daily basis. Anyone can pick a fight and verbalize her anger. This sort of reaction does not necessitate exercising any restraint or self-control. However, to truly operate in love and to control your spirit are signs of great spiritual strength and maturity.

Proverbs 17:14 avers:

> *"The beginning of strife is as when one letteth out water: therefore leave off contention, before it be meddled with."*

When you feel that desire to wade into an argument, why not let love govern your response instead of allowing the spirit of strife to loose a flood tide of destructive emotions into your home? Mohandas Gandhi said, "Love is the subtlest force in the world." Are there power struggles and a continual tug-of-war taking place in your home? The solution is simple—love more and more and you will fight less and less. "Love is a game that two can play and both win" (Eva Gabor). Wouldn't it be much more refreshing to live in a loving environment instead of strife-filled surroundings? Use the key of love—it will unlock the door to happiness and wisdom.

"The art of being wise is the art of knowing what to over-look" (William James). "Love is the healer, the reconciler, the inspirer, the creator. . . ." (Rosemary Haughton).

John 3:16 states:

> *"For God so loved the world, that he gave. . . ."*

When the principles of love are established in a home, they will bring an awareness of one another's needs. These loving precepts will create an environment in which giving to those we love becomes the focus rather than our seeking for our own fulfillment. This in turn will cause the one who loves to receive greater emotional fulfillment because, as Marjory Stoneman Douglas said it so well, "Love is a multiplication."

Recently during a conversation concerning our need to practice the love of God, someone challenged me about whether they had to love certain people whom they didn't consider their "brethren." However, this attitude is also dealt with in Matthew 5:43-48:

> *"Ye have heard that it hath been said, Thou shalt love thy neighbour, and hate thine enemy. But I say unto you, **Love your enemies, bless them that curse you, do good to them that hate you, and pray for them which despitefully use you, and persecute you**; that ye may be the children of your Father which is in heaven: for he maketh his sun to rise on the evil and on the good, and sendeth rain on the just and on the unjust. For if ye love them which love you, what reward have ye? do not even the publicans the same? And if ye salute your brethren only, what do ye more than others? do not even the publicans so? Be ye therefore perfect, even as your Father which is in heaven is perfect."*

Talk about settling the question of whom we are to love! God's Word leaves no loopholes for hateful habits. Love for our enemies, as well as for our family and friends, illustrates the effectual divine nature at work in our lives. "To return evil for good is devilish; to return good for good is human; to return good for evil is God-like." When we learn to play by the rule book of

God's love, everyone becomes a winner. "Let love be purified, and all the rest will follow. A pure love is thus, indeed, the panacea for all the ills of the world" (Henry David Thoreau).

The third elemental teaching which must be taught in our homes is "holiness with sobriety" which literally means our holy lifestyle is to be coupled with wisdom and self-control. A lack of wisdom and inability to control ourselves will destroy our testimony and taint the beauty of our separation. Often I have seen those who major on making sure the outward man is in total keeping with the Word of God while at the same time destroying others with their gossiping tongues. Nothing is more unattractive than seeing a Pentecostal person who looks good on the outside but manifests an awful attitude from the inside.

One of my friends told me about being at a restaurant with some of his ministerial colleagues. During the course of the meal, one of the men treated their waitress in a very unchristian manner. It was quite embarrassing to my friend, not to mention the destructive impact it had on their testimony. Do we show the world a proper reflection of self-controlled holiness, or is our testimony tainted by unwise actions? Furthermore, what kind of mixed messages are we establishing in our homes and churches? Will our children grow up and embrace the beauty of holiness, or will they be turned off by hypocrisy at home? Many things factor into our composite witness as the following piece of prudent guidance illustrates:

> *A man is known by his . . .*
> *Character—what he is.*
> *Conversation—what he says.*
> *Conduct—what he does.*
> *Contribution—what he gives.*
> *Creed—what he believes.*

Holiness is so much more than just the correctness of our external appearance. It is also manifested by our inner attitudes and outward actions. May our walk and our talk line up as we model and teach becoming behavior within our world, in private as well as in the public view. The choices we make and lives we live will have a profound effect for generations to come. Personally, I never ceased to be thankful for the teachings which were instilled in my life from the time of childhood. One of the greatest things my mother gave to our family was her example of consistent and faithful Christianity. God was always first in our home, and prayer resounded daily within our four walls. Unselfish giving of time, money, and ministry was a way of life for our family.

I never realized the profound power of this sort of teaching upon my life until I was in a state of crisis. One Sunday morning after my world came crashing in, the phone rang. Little did I realize the verbal abuse that was about to issue forth upon me. After hanging up the phone, I was literally reeling from the shock of the attack, almost to the point of hysteria. For one of the first times in my life, I didn't want to go to church. At that insane moment, my first instinct was to run and to hide from this horrible state called life. However, in that moment of despair, the remembrance of my mother's consistent faithfulness was like an anchor in the midst of the storm. Suddenly, I knew there was no room for quarter. The only rational choice was to make my way to the house of God. There were two little pairs of eyes watching my reaction and resultant decisions, and those decisions would have a profound, eternal effect on my two daughters. At that moment, godly determination swept over me, steeling my resolve to remain steadfast even during this dark hour. Giving up, staying home, and letting unfaithfulness creep in were not options. My precious mother was such a wise woman teacher, and her godly instruction kept me stead-fast in the faith when all was reeling and rocking in my world. Thank you, Mom, for teaching me to value truth, to love others, and to embrace true holiness. Your wise teachings are being passed on from generation to generation. Mother, I rise up and call you blessed! **Oh, the power of a wise woman teacher!**

Likewise, the future of succeeding generations is hanging in the balance. The choices you make today will determine the choices they will make tomorrow. Will you answer the call to become a wise woman teacher of good things?

$\mathcal{M}$en $\mathcal{A}$re
LIKE WHAT?

"... to love their husbands, ..."

"A wife who is in competition with her husband, or who has just enough mind to detect his faults, is the extinguisher of genius." ~ *Goethe*

In Titus 2:4, Paul included the necessity of loving their husbands in the list of godly women's duties. On the surface, that would seem to be a no-brainer. However, the question arises, Do women truly know what it means to love their husbands? One of the most common errors made by women is their failure to understand the difference between the male and female psyche. This lack of understanding is many times the root cause for rocky marital relationships. The ability to truly love your husband will necessitate the acquisition of understanding about the inner workings of the male mind-set.

In her excellent book, *The Proper Care and Feeding of Husbands*, Dr. Laura Schlessinger details the male/female differences which begin to take place within the womb:

"The differences between men and women begin in the womb. At first, all fetus' brains are virtually the same. At about nine weeks of gestation, though, testosterone surges through the male (XY) fetus, changing the direction of general development toward masculinity.

"With respect to communication, the result of those differences are apparent early on in childhood. Studies in child care development have documented behavioral differences in children even in the first year. In one study, a barrier was placed between the child and his or her mother. The boys, wanting to get back to Mommy, try to get around or over the barrier, or they try to knock it down. The male response is physical, and it's aimed at solving the problem. The female children, on the other hand, verbalized their distress, and their mommies came and picked them up. The female response is verbal.

"As children grow up, parents notice that their daughters are unbelievably verbal and usually prone to high drama. These same parents notice that their sons are 'men of few words' but lots of action. Obviously, within the populations of both men and women, there is variation; nonetheless these generalizations exist for a reason: They represent the larger population and reveal some focal points of problems between husbands and wives trying to communicate in a manner that enhances the husband and the wife as well as the marriage."

As this preceding excerpt points out, communication styles is one of the major differences between men and women. For the most part, the majority of women do not have any problem giving voice to their emotions and opinions. It is not uncommon for them to resort to whining complaint as a form of communication. This sort of habitual complaining can even become a source of unhealthy entertainment with their girlfriends where marital grievances are aired and the male species discredited. Countless times I have heard women talk in a somewhat pretentious manner about their ability to cut their husbands down to size. Sadly, what many fail to realize is they are possibly doing irreparable damage to their marriages.

Conversely, men tend to suffer in silence long before they will complain or voice their inner pain. Actually, the male mentality is very uncomplicated—they usually say what they mean and mean what they say. Their basic necessities are quite simple and include direct communication, respect, appreciation, food, and good lovin'. If these needs are met, a fulfilled man will do all in his power to please his wife. Lamentably, instead of focusing on pleasing the person who should be the most important to them, some women will put more time and effort into impressing total strangers. One of Dr. Laura's listeners, Gary, says, "A husband is like a horse. At the end of the day he is usually rode hard and put away sweaty. Like in the movies, if his master drives and beats him, he'll go just so far before bucking and rebelling. If you love him, if you coax him, he'll drive himself till his heart explodes before he will let down his master. He'll give himself to death for the one he loves. Which way should a woman handle a man?" "Men are born of women and spend the rest of their lives yearning for a woman's acceptance and approval" (Dr. Laura).

Again, I tap into more of the composite male insight, voiced by yet another of Dr. Laura's listeners, Dan, who summed up the male mind quite well, "I am a thirty-seven-year-old man who has seen quite a bit of life, and I can offer this to your search for how to treat a man. We are men, not dumb-dumbs, psychics, or one bit unromantic. We need only clear communication, appreciation, honest love, and respect. This will be repaid by laying the moon and stars at your feet for your pleasure. There is no need to 'work' a man to get what you want. We live to take care of a wife, family, and home. Just remember that we are men, and know that our needs are simple but not to be ignored. A good man is hard to find, not to keep."

Recently, I was privileged to attend a very informative lecture given by Dr. John Thurman, a Christian therapist and teacher in our area. During the course of the evening, he spoke quite candidly about the importance of marital relationships. At one point, Dr. Thurman gave a very humorous analogy concerning the male species which I would like to relate to you. He said, "Men are like dogs. They need someone to feed them, play with them, and to pat them on the head and say, 'Good boy!'" At that point, the entire audience erupted into laughter as the wise doctor went on to explain his enlightening theory. Please bear in mind this was a man saying this about himself and his fellow compatriots.

Although countless books have been written on the subject of marriage, for the sake of our continuing study, let us take a brief look at these three basic areas of male need. The first thing men need is someone to feed them. When considering this topic of feeding your man, I was reminded of an old cookbook my mother used to have when I was growing up. Simply entitled *The Way to a Man's Heart*, the book's cover was adorned with hearts and women dressed in cooking ensembles. It was reminiscent of the old saying, "The quickest way to a man's heart is through his stomach." Actually, the area of feeding your husband encompasses more than just making meals. It includes the whole art of housekeeping and creating an inviting environment for the man of the house to enjoy.

When a man comes home weary from a long day on the job, nothing is more inviting than walking into a well-ordered home, filled with the aroma of a delicious dinner and being greeted by a loving, attentive wife. Unfortunately, many women make the age-old mistake of waiting for their husbands to get home so they can dump all their dilemmas at the men's feet the minute they walk through the door. Nothing could be more of a turn-off, especially if the wife is still in her bathrobe, the house is in disarray, and the kids are screaming. A wise woman knows some things must take priority if her marriage is to going to flourish. These priorities include making sure she is well-groomed, along with straightening the house, tending to the children, and putting together a nice dinner. Furthermore, wisdom says it is better to wait until a more opportune time to discuss difficult issues with her man.

At this point, some women may feel I am being unrealistic. However, it is all a matter of planning your day and prioritizing your duties. Your walk with God should always be first and foremost because real love can only come as a direct result of a sacred relationship with Jesus Christ. When God is number one, this will set the stage for a divine romance within your marriage that comes straight from the heart of the Creator. True intimacy within your marriage may only be achieved when you allow God to have total access to your heart. Next on your list of priorities should be your relationship with your spouse, and this union must take precedence over all other earthly relationships. Your marital responsibilities should always supersede any other familial duties. If you place your children or other family members before your husband, everyone will suffer because this is not the proper order for a home. A man's house should be his castle, and he should **always** be treated as the king of the castle.

I have never met a man yet who did not enjoy coming home to a wonderful, home-cooked meal served attractively in a clean house. After his day of diligent labor, don't you think your husband deserves a show of loving gratitude for providing for his family? Wouldn't it be nice to make his favorite meal and serve it by candlelight? What if you met your husband at the door with a kiss, then brought him the paper and a cold drink while you finished making dinner? Do you think it might improve the climate of your marriage? His loving response might surprise you.

Moving on to the second area of need in a man's life, Dr. Thurman's analogy identified it as someone to "play" with him. I would imagine most of my readers' minds are immediately focusing on the obvious sphere of sexual interaction. That is, of course, the first and foremost need of a man. Nevertheless, this next arena of necessity embraces a larger range of romantic involvement than just the sexual act. There are many ways to enjoy your mate, which in turn will cause the intimacy of your marriage to flourish.

Along with the strong male need for sexual fulfillment is the desire for recreational companionship. Men enjoy being with a woman who will share activities with them such as golfing, hiking, fishing, hunting, etc. When a woman cultivates an interest in hobbies her husband enjoys doing, this creates a strong bond of shared interest, which in turn fosters a deeper level of affection. Far too often we women tend to focus on doing things that interest us, such as shopping, crafting, or reading. However, it would be a wonderful marital boon if we took time to cultivate mutual activities that could be enjoyed with our spouses. How about taking a daily twilight walk as you both talk about the events of the day? Why not go on a fishing trip together or find a pastime both would enjoy doing?

Continuing in this vein of thought, have you ever considered taking the time to romance your husband? For the most part, our society has laid the "burden" of creating romantic scenarios on the shoulders of the man; still, there is nothing more invigorating than planning an unexpected idyllic encounter for your man. "Life is a romantic business, but you have to make the romance" (Oliver Wendell Holmes).

In her excellent book, entitled *Romancing Your Husband—Enjoying a Passionate Life Together*, Debra White Smith outlines several excellent ideas for exciting encounters with your mate. Her suggestions vary from simple, spontaneous, and loving gestures to more elaborate dates and weekend getaways. Whether you have been married for two, twenty, or forty years, it is never too late to spice up your marital relationship. How about sending your husband a loving card every day for the next seven days? Or why not call him and ask him out for a romantic date? Put a love note under his pillow or on the seat of his car. Let your imagination soar as you rekindle the flame of passion for one another.

The placement of the Song of Solomon within the pages of Holy Writ is divine evidence of God's intense desire for His people to cultivate a passionate marital relationship. Hebrews 13:4 avows:

> *"Marriage is honourable in all, and the bed undefiled: but whoremongers and adulterers God will judge."*

A sexually healthy marriage is God's idea. Unfortunately, the world has tried to taint and to pervert this sacred union. After all, to be attractive to your spouse and attracted by your spouse is truly honorable and holy in the sight of God. A godly marriage should be the most exhilarating alliance on earth.

"Love gives itself; it is not bought" (Henry Wadsworth Longfellow). Take the time to enjoy your mate, because your loving relationship is a gift from God Himself. It is so important to cherish the most important person in your own private universe. "Love and you shall be loved. All love is mathematical, just as much as the two sides of an algebraic equation"

(Ralph Waldo Emerson). "Couples who play together stay together" (Paul Pearsall).

The third area we will examine in this chapter is a man's need to be respected. Ephesians 5:33 admonishes the woman to "reverence" her husband:

> *"Nevertheless let every one of you in particular*
> *so love his wife even as himself; and the wife*
> *see that she reverence her husband."*

The Amplified Bible says it in this manner, "Let the wife see that she respects and reverences her husband [that she notices him, regards him, honors him, prefers him, venerates and esteems him; and that she defers to him, praises him, and loves and admires him exceedingly]." This seemingly small word "reverence" includes quite a list of responsibilities.

In light of the woman's responsibility to "reverence" her husband, here are some questions for your consideration: Do you notice your husband in an admiring way? How long has it been since you complimented him? Is the law of kindness in your tongue, or have you found yourself falling in the proverbial trap of engaging in sarcastic jesting at the expense of your marriage partner? This common behavioral mistake was so aptly illustrated in a catalog advertising a holiday T-shirt and matching cap which read "3 Wise Men? [Be Serious]." How many women would see that and chuckle, when in reality this brand of so-called humor is not really amusing but rather abusing. Proverbs 14:1 speaks of the constructive and destructive power which a woman wields within her home:

> *"Every wise woman buildeth her house: but the*
> *foolish plucketh it down with her hands."*

"Kind words can be short and easy to speak, but their echoes are truly endless" (Mother Teresa).

St. Teresa of Avila advised, "Accustom yourself continually to make many acts of love, for they enkindle and melt the soul." Do you defer to his desires, or does the world have to revolve around what you want to do? How long has it been since you took time to show a genuine interest in your husband's work? Are you a safe place where he can unburden himself and share his deepest fears or emotions? Would the following verse be a true expression of the gentle safety of your love?

Let my love be like a pillow
you rest your heart upon.
Soft and giving, supportive and yielding.
Let my love be like a coverlet
that forever wraps around you.
Soft and giving, comforting and warm.
Come walk along love's path with me,
Your hand in mine, husband and wife.
Come be my loyal traveling mate
Along the open road of life.

In preparation for writing her book, *For Women Only—What You Need to Know About the Inner Lives of Men*, Shaunti Feldhahn interviewed more than a thousand men from CEOs to security guards. After assessing the results of her extensive survey, she found that 74 percent of the men interviewed would rather be alone and unloved than to feel inadequate and disrespected. Mrs. Feldhahn's findings affirm the importance of adhering to the apostle Paul's admonition to reverence your husband. Shaunti emphatically states in her new book, "If you want to love your man in the way he needs to be loved, then you need to ensure that he feels your respect most of all. If a man feels disrespected, he is going to feel unloved."

The following are four key areas in which we can demonstrate respect to our husbands:

1. **Respect his judgment:** This involves valuing his opinions and decisions. It means to refrain from telling him what to do. When you order him around like one of the kids, your husband is belittled in an extreme manner. Showing trust in his decision-making abilities is another way to demonstrate your respect for him.

2. **Respect his abilities:** Men like to figure things out for themselves. If we try to help them or tell them how to do things, this is oftentimes viewed as distrust in their ability to accomplish a task. Yes, it is definitely true that men like to find their way to a predetermined destination without asking for directions, because it makes them feel as if they have conquered something. Men love it when we support them and let them figure things out. In essence we are saying, "I know you can do it!" This kind of trust in their abilities will ignite their passion to succeed.

3. **Respect in communication:** This involves not only what we say but how we say it. For instance, if your husband wants to try to repair something at your house and you tell him he is not really a "fix-it" man, the words can be extremely devastating to his ego. What may seem like an offhand remark to you could actually be quite damaging. Would you want your husband to tease you about gaining weight? In the same manner, they do not like to be teased or spoken to in a way that makes them feel inadequate.

4. **Respect in public:** Public criticism of your husband or questioning his judgment in front of others is very demeaning. One man said, "My wife says things about me in public that she considers teasing. I consider them torture." The male ego is very fragile, and unfortunately some women feel it is their calling in life to cut their men down to size. In reality, the male ego is the driving force that enables a man to accomplish his duties as the provider and protector of his family. Build up your husband — don't tear him down. Praise him in public as well as in private. Let the world know you value, esteem, and delight in your husband.

Recently, I heard a charming story concerning the active preservation of a long and happy marriage. After celebrating fifty years of wedded bliss, the happy couple was asked to share their secret of marital longevity. The man said it was because he always tried to be unselfish since there is no "I" in marriage. The woman responded that her secret for success was that she never corrected her husband's spelling. While you may be chuckling at this humorous anecdote, there is much to be said for the underlying truth of this little tale. "Your spouse is your closest relative and is entitled to depend on you as a common ally, supporter, and champion" (Aaron Beck).

Goethe said, "Love does not dominate; it cultivates." According to *Webster's Dictionary*, cultivate means "to improve and prepare, to grow or tend, to form and refine as by education, to seek the good will of." Just as a flower garden or a wheat field has to be cultivated in order for the owner to enjoy the benefit of beauty and bread, a wonderful marriage is produced through diligent effort. "Love dies only when growth stops" (Pearl Buck).

The Art of Marriage

A good marriage must be created.
In the marriage the little things are the
big things . . .
It is never being too old to hold hands.
It is remembering to say "I love you"
at least once a day.
It is never going to sleep angry.
It is having a mutual sense of values
and common objectives.
It is standing together facing the world.
It is forming a circle of love that gathers in
the whole family.
It is speaking words of appreciation and
demonstrating gratitude in thoughtful ways.
It is having the capacity to forgive and forget.
It is giving each other an atmosphere
in which each can grow.
It is a common search for the good
and the beautiful.
It is not only marrying the right person—
it is being the right partner.

~ Wilferd A. Peterson

Marriages are made in heaven, but they must be maintained on earth. "When love and skill work together, expect a masterpiece" (John Ruskin). Love is a decision. Why not decide today to love your husband in a greater measure than ever before? Determine to build a continual aura of romance, excitement, and expectation in your marriage. In response to the question posed by this chapter—Men are like what?—they are a wonderful creation formed by the hand of God, and they need to be nurtured, needed, reverenced, and romanced. Love your husband and allow him to be your lover, your confidante, and your best friend.

> *Lover, mentor, teacher, friend,*
> *My love for you shall never end.*
> *Companion, healer, partner, guide,*
> *Forever I'll be by your side.*

> *True love is found when*
> *two hearts are going in the same*
> *direction, at a similar pace,*
> *with a compatible outlook.*

Recommended Reading:

Feldhahn, Shaunti. *For Women Only—What You Need to Know About the Inner Lives of Men*. Sisters, OR: Multnomah Publishers.

Harley, Willard F., Jr. *His Needs, Her Needs—Building an Affair Proof Marriage*. Grand Rapids, MI: Baker House Books.

Rosberg, Dr. Gary and Barbara. *40 Unforgettable Dates with Your Mate—Creative Ways to Meet the Love Needs of Husbands and Wives*. Wheaton, IL: Tyndale House Publishers.

Schlessinger, Dr. Laura. *The Proper Care and Feeding of Husbands*. New York, NY: Harper Collins Publishers.

Smith, Debra White. *Romancing Your Husband—Enjoying a Passionate Life Together*. Eugene, OR: Harvest House Publishers.

Thomas, Gary. *Sacred Marriage*. Grand Rapids, MI: Zondervan.

Motherhood's LASTING LEGACY

". . . to love their children, . . ."

"An ounce of mother is worth a pound of clergy."
~ Spanish proverb

Sitting on a shelf above my desk is a little stained-glass plaque given to me by my girls. Inscribed with the following poem, it illustrates the lasting influence of a mother:

> *To one who bears the sweetest name,*
> *And adds luster to the same,*
> *Long life to her,*
> *For there's no other*
> *Who takes the place of my Dear Mother.*

Webster's Dictionary defines the word **mother** as "a female parent, to give birth to, to be the mother of, to care for; nourish and protect." Close on the heels of loving our husbands comes the responsibility to love our children. Perhaps no other occupation has such long lasting, even eternal consequences. Today's society has downplayed the importance of motherhood to the point of creating, in some cases, almost a sneering disdain for this God-given, womanly role. A former President's wife mockingly referred to the opposing candidate's wife as someone who made chocolate chip cookies for her children. In her eyes, a maternal activity of this nature was considered beneath her superior capabilities, when in reality, a mother will have a far greater impact on the world than any other person. One of America's foremost Presidents, Abraham Lincoln, gave this tribute to his beloved mother, "All that I am or ever hope to be, I owe to my angel mother." In the same vein, America's inaugural President, George Washington, declared, "My mother was the most beautiful woman I ever saw. All I am I owe to my mother. I attribute all my success in life to the moral, intellectual, and physical education I received from her."

Oftentimes women fail to realize the extreme effect they have on their environment. A mother does not just birth children; she is bringing forth eternal souls. Immortal processes are set in motion with the birth of each baby, thereby compounding the great tragedy of people engaging in illicit relationships which produce illegitimate children. All children, whether conceived in legitimacy or illegitimacy, will live forever, and each mother will have a profound impact on the impending destiny of these children. It is so vital for mothers to realize their duties are much more far-reaching than wiping nasty noses, changing dirty diapers, washing soiled laundry, making yet another peanut butter and jelly sandwich, or picking up countless toys. Motherhood's lasting legacy continues into eternity and can produce life or death, salvation or destruction, heaven or hell in the lives of their offspring. When looking into the eyes of your precious posterity, take a moment to ponder the momentous power of your influence. Through the daily interaction with your children, your fingerprints are leaving enduring impressions upon eternity.

Mother, you carved no shapeless marble
to some high soul design;
But with a finer sculpture you shaped
this soul of mine.
You built no great cathedrals
that centuries applaud;
But with a grace exquisite
your life cathedraled God.

~ Thomas Fessenden

Choosing to liken the church to a mother in Galatians 4:26, the Almighty validates the intrinsic role of motherhood:

> *"But Jerusalem which is above is free, which is the mother of us all."*

Furthermore, Genesis 3:20 identifies the first woman, Eve, as the "mother of all living":

> *"And Adam called his wife's name Eve; because she was the mother of all living."*

As has already been stated in chapter four of this book, our original mother's influence continues to have extensive eternal impact even to this present day. The success of every family unit is vitally dependent upon the mother.

Truly, the child's relationship with his or her mother will affect so many other relationships throughout life. A boy's interaction with his mother will determine how he treats his future wife and daughters. If there is an unhealthy relationship between a man and his mother, chances are very great he will have difficulty relating to his wife. According to Dr. James Hughes, a minister's interaction with his congregation and even his ability to pastor will also be directly impacted by his maternal relationship. This means a mother's influence can actually reach out and touch an entire congregation for either good or bad. Talk about far-reaching consequences!

Through the years, I have observed men who were deeply wounded by their mothers during childhood's formative years. Without fail, it seems there is an emotional crippling which takes great effort to overcome. Tragically, this can even send some men down a destructive pathway of seeking for female affirmation through multiple adulterous liaisons. One man in particular who had suffered emotional, verbal, and physical abuse at the hand of his mother confessed his hatred for women. His mother's inhumane treatment caused him to view women as nothing more than sexual objects to be used for the gratification of his erotic desires. With each illicit affair, he was driven, so it seemed, to vicariously attain the approval his mother had withheld from him. Sadly, his emotional neediness could never be satisfied in this manner. It only served to destroy him, his marriage, and his life.

Another man among my acquaintances was forever impacted when his mother deserted their family. Standing on the verge of manhood, he tearfully begged his mother not to leave, then watched in horror as she selfishly walked away. In order to cope with the painful rejection, his heart was hardened, and through the years the ability to forgive became a very difficult issue for him. Even after becoming very successful in life, he had locked inside a very painful memory of the past, which colored his entire outlook and interaction with others.

Two men in particular told me how their mothers gave them coal in their Christmas stockings. Even though the incident took place years earlier, it still rankled within them and caused a continued feeling of inadequacy in other areas of their lives. It seemed no matter how hard they strove to excel, the niggling notion of their mother's rejection never quite faded away.

Many times when men are insanely jealous or controlling of their wives, the root cause can be traced back to the insecurity of their maternal relationship. Traumatic childhood experiences such as seeing their mother abused or involved with numerous men can induce this sort of response in men. By nature men are protective; however, if they are privy to inappropriate sexual scenarios, the proper responses can be short-circuited during the formative and impressionable childhood years.

The biblical narrative of Rebekah and Jacob stands in testament to the powerful influence of a mother. Engaging in the destructive cycle of playing favorites, she induced her son to deceive his father so as to obtain the patriarchal blessing. Her blatant disregard for her husband's leadership necessitated Jacob's flight for his life in the face of Esau's jealous rage. Meanwhile, during Jacob's sojourn in Padan-Aram, he became entangled in his uncle Laban's deceptive behavior, which seemed to be a family trait. In the end, only a life-altering, name-changing angelic wrestling match could free Jacob from the debilitating maternal influence of his past. In order to become Israel, the prevailing prince, he had to go through great striving to overcome the ingrained deceptive tendencies which had been bequeathed by name and birth and then instilled within by his mother's unseemly instruction.

In like manner, girls are also profoundly impacted by their mothers' actions. One lady told a sordid story of suffering sexual abuse at the hands of numerous men all under the condoning eye of her mother. In fact, the mother was completely privy to this horrid, reprehensible activity both by allowing it and even by encouraging it. Later, this girl grew into a woman who was easily victimized and seemed unable to interact appropriately with the men in her life. Driven by her desire for male approval and love, she became a victim of others' lust.

When a girl does not have the loving example of a godly mother, her upbringing can have a direct bearing on her ability to show proper love and affection for her own children. Furthermore, when girls see their mothers treat their fathers inappropriately, this can set the stage for their own marital deficiencies. If a woman is unsubmissive to her husband, her children will suffer the consequences. It can cause boys to dislike women and girls to distrust men. It would behoove us to seriously consider the lasting legacy of motherhood.

On the other hand, a godly mother can equip her children to be successful in every area of life. Andrew Jackson's testimony bears witness to this profound truth, "There never was a woman like her. She was gentle as a dove and brave as a lioness. . . The memory of my mother and her teachings were, after all, the only capital I had to start life with, and on that capital I have made my way."

A mother who prays for her children and validates their worth will reap a harvest of blessed dividends as her children rise up and call her blessed. "Youth fades; love droops, the leaves of friendship fall; a mother's secret hope outlives them all" (Oliver Wendell Holmes). Booker T. Washington, the college president who against all odds established Tuskegee Institute and became a man who profoundly affected our world, had this to say about his mother, "In all my efforts to learn to read, my mother shared fully my ambition and sympathized with me and aided me in every way she could. If I have done anything in life worth attention, I feel sure that I inherited the disposition from my mother."

"While my father was the one to present God to me as a heavenly Father who tenderly cared about each one of His children, it was my mother who showed me how a relationship with Him could change everyday situations" (Catherine Marshall). Because of a woman's spiritual sensitivity, she has the ability to model and instill within her family a passionate desire for the things of God. Indelibly impressed upon my mind are the sacred recollections of my own mother's prayers. Hearing her melodious voice raised in vibrant praise along with her skilled and anointed piano playing is also a precious memory which colors the fabric of my life and walk with God. How thankful I am for her legacy of lasting consecration! To this present time, my mother remains steadfast, immovable, always abounding in the work of the Lord even during her latter years. Mother, once again I rise up and call you blessed. "Of all the rights of women, the greatest is to be a mother" (Lin Yutang).

The following poem could come straight from the heart of every loving mother:

I Loved You Enough

Someday when my children are old enough to
understand the logic that motivates a parent
I will tell them:

I loved you enough to ask where you were going,
With whom, and what time you would be home.

I loved you enough to insist that you save money
and buy a bike for yourself
Even though we could afford to buy one for you.

BECOMING BEHAVIOR

I loved you enough to be silent
and let you discover
That your new friend was a creep.

I loved you enough to make you take the Milky Way
back to the store (with a bite out of it)
and tell the clerk,
"I stole this yesterday and I want to pay for it."

I loved you enough to stand over you for two hours
while you cleaned your room,
A job that would have taken me fifteen minutes.

I loved you enough to let you see anger,
disappointment, and tears in my eyes.
Children must learn that their parents
aren't perfect.

I loved you enough to let you assume
responsibility for your actions
Even when the penalties were so harsh
that they almost broke my heart.

But, most of all, I loved you enough to say NO
when I knew you would hate me for it.
Those were the most difficult battles of all.
I'm glad I won them, because in the end,
you won too.

~ Author unknown

In light of the profound effect of each mother, the United States instituted a national day of celebration to commemorate their contributions to our world. The following facts tell about the initial establishment of this special holiday:

In 1908 Ana Jarvis, from Grafton, West Virginia, began a campaign to establish a national Mother's Day. Persuading her mother's church in Grafton, West Virginia, to celebrate Mother's Day on the anniversary of her mother's death, a memorial service was held there on May 10, 1908. When Jarvis moved to Philadelphia the following year, another day of commemoration took place in her new area of residence. In their quest to establish a national Mother's Day, Jarvis and others also began a letter-writing campaign to ministers, businessmen, and politicians, which was successful. In 1914, President Woodrow Wilson made the official announcement proclaiming Mother's Day a national observance that was to be held each year on the second Sunday of May.

Traditionally, Mother's Day is one of the most widely celebrated events in our nation. On May's second Sunday, restaurants are filled to overflowing, florists and card companies do a booming business, and the telephone wires come alive as children seek to remember the women who gave them life.

Hundreds of dewdrops to greet the dawn,
Hundreds of bees in the purple clover,
Hundreds of butterflies on the lawn,
But only one mother the wide world over.

~ George Cooper

As this chapter draws to a close, I beg you, the reader, to once again consider the utterly immense influence you exert as a mother. You are more than just a female parent. During pregnancy, your body houses an eternal soul. After the birth, you are caring for, protecting, and nourishing lives that will possibly impact history, the world, or God's kingdom. Next time you are tempted to downplay your role in the scheme of life, just remember you touch eternity each time a diaper is changed, a nose is wiped, a sandwich is made, a bedtime story is read, or a nightly prayer is prayed. You are God's hands to imprint His purposes upon successive generations. Your son could be another David, Daniel, Samuel, Joseph, Peter, or Paul. Maybe, just maybe that little girl of yours could grow into an Esther, a Hannah, an Abigail, a Jochebed, a Miriam, or a Mary who changes the course of history for all time.

> *"Lo, children are an heritage of the LORD: and the fruit of the womb is his reward. As arrows are in the hand of a mighty man; so are children of the youth. Happy is the man that hath his quiver full of them: they shall not be ashamed, but they shall speak with the enemies in the gate" (Psalm 127:3-5).*

> *"Thy wife shall be as a fruitful vine by the sides of thine house: thy children like olive plants round about thy table" (Psalm 128:3).*

May your children be as arrows in the hands of the Lord to bring down the forces of the enemy. May they flourish as fruitful plants in the house of God! Perform your duties well as a mother. Eternity is depending on you!

M *is for the million things she gave me.*
O *means only that she's growing old.*
T *is for the tears she shed to save me;*
H *is for her heart of purest gold.*
E *is for her eyes with love light shining.*
R *means right, and right she'll always be.*

Put them all together: they spell MOTHER, the word that means the world to me!

Passage
OF PURITY

". . . to be discreet, chaste, . . ."

"If you think you're too small to make a difference, you haven't been in bed with a mosquito." ~ Anita Roddick

Whether perusing a fashion catalog, combing through a clothing rack at a local emporium, or checking the ads in the store windows at the mall, the two words **discreet** and **chaste** are definitely not the first adjectives which come to mind. In a world which has been paralyzed by impurity, discretion and chastity are no longer held in high esteem. This is incessantly evidenced by the media's bombardment upon our sensitivities. Continually, women are encouraged to "bare all." What's more, the advice, "If you've got it, flaunt it, girl!" seems to sway many girls' clothing choices. Advertising backless, strapless, low-cut, see-through matrimonial attire, even bridal magazines, it appears, are in on the collusion to undress women in the public arena. Ironically, the white wedding dress, which is supposed to be synonymous with chaste purity, has actually become yet another excuse to expose one's body. Many times, even Christian girls seem to buy into the notion that it is okay to show off some flesh during their nuptial festivities.

Narcissism rules the fashion arena as bare legs and cleavage spill out everywhere. Once while waiting in a doctor's office, out of curiosity I picked up a fashion magazine which was touting ways to catch a man. After skimming quickly through the article, I realized it could be summarized rather quickly: "Take off your clothes and wear makeup." This sensual advice was actually encouraging women to engage in a form of "legal" prostitution. If you think my response is a bit overactive, I would ask you to stop to think about what streetwalkers do in order to entice their clientele. They paint their faces and wear abbreviated clothing designed to arouse the male libido. Nevertheless, even with immodesty swirling all around, it is imperative for ladies to take their cues from God's Word instead of from *Cosmopolitan* or *Glamour* magazines.

An interesting essay entitled "Loosely Tied Strings" uncovers the double standard many fall prey to concerning the governing of our offspring's attire. It reads as follows:

"Her back, covered only by a couple of loosely tied strings, demanded attention—and got it. A group of admirers voiced their approval of the girl's backless bandanna top and shorts. She seemed oblivious to the comments thrown in her direction, but no doubt she received their message. The above scene could easily be from the teen scene at a local mall. But, in reality, the girl was five: and her admirers were her mom's friends. The setting was a church function.

"Because our culture glorifies appearance and emphasizes sex appeal, we must address this issue with our children from an early age. If we want our teenagers and adult children to reflect godly morals in their dress, we must lay godly foundations when they are young.

"As Christians, our standards come from God's Word, not from pop culture. Excessive exposure to sexual material has desensitized the church. Everywhere we look, we see people in various stages of undress. From lingerie advertisements to fellow shoppers, we see it all."

As the previous excerpt reveals, oftentimes the breakdown of purity can start at an early age. It is alarming to see the clothing children and young people are allowed to wear in our churches, at our youth camps, and during conferences. Walls of chastity and discretion are being demolished on every side. This was so profoundly illustrated to me during an episode that took place during a youth function. On this particular occasion, I watched in horrified amazement as a young girl running by a group of boys pulled up her skirt until the side split opened and exposed her upper thighs. Seemingly without an ounce of shame, she deliberately uncovered her flesh in front of these young men. After passing the group of guys, the skirt was lowered to a more modest length. Honestly, the incident left me practically speechless and made me wonder whether the principles of purity are being passed to our posterity. Are we teaching our young women to be discreet and chaste?[1]

It seems our entire culture is centered on instilling the art of seduction into our women and girls. In her book *Dress Code*, Toby Fischer-Mirkin has a chapter entitled "Fashion Seduction: Sex Appeal and Style." Throughout this particular portion of her book, she defines various and sundry styles which enhance sensuality. Please allow me to share just a few of her secular fashion insights for your consideration:

"Whatever her motives, a woman will always have an abundance of seductive clothing from which to choose. Each season the fashion industry creates alluring new fashions intended for 'the eye of the beholder,' whether it's a strapless dress that exposes gleaming bare shoulders, a plunging neckline that shows off the shadows of cleavage, or a backless blouse that draws the eye to the sinuous curve of the back and spine. The truth of the matter is that revealing fashions make a woman feel sexually attractive. Navel-skimming sweaters, thigh-high hemlines, and thong swimsuits are essential props in the quest for sexual satisfaction. But are you aware of what other messages these overt clothes send?

"When we wear provocative clothing, our body language is subtly altered. Walking and moving in such styles changes a woman's posture, endowing each movement with a seductive, contrived air. When we wear body-conscious clothing, we divert attention from our faces to our bodies. Clinging clothing molds, lifts, and thrusts out our body parts, unlike softer, draped clothing, which draws attention to our face.

"A wrap sweater in Lycra or another clinging fabric makes a more overt sexual statement, caressing the body as it divides and lifts the breasts. Among the most titillating garments are those that invite the viewer to linger on a particular part of the body. Often they both cover and reveal at the same time. Revealing a little is, and always has been, much more tantalizing than baring everything. A long dress that caresses our curves and has a plunging back or a slit up the side is much more interesting to the eye than a short, clinging Lycra dress.

"Men have always found the flash of a curvaceous limb titillating. Historically, short skirts, and even those exposing only glimpses of the leg, were reserved for women on public view—prostitutes and showgirls. The deeply slit evening dress is another provocative look. Men's eyes are drawn immediately to the side of the dress as they follow the slit to the top of the wearer's thigh; they may never even notice the rest of the gown.

"Breasts are probably the single most potent symbol of female power and sexuality, and they're literally popping up and out on fashion runways and the pages of slick magazines.

Flashing one's breasts by unbuttoning the top buttons of a blouse is a gesture of sexual assertion and may also be a way of conveying that one is proud to be a woman."

And so on and so forth . . . Having written about this topic in more detail in my previous books, I do not want to be redundant on this subject; however, Ms. Fischer's fashion insights are particularly interesting in the light of our study concerning discretion and chastity. If we wear these types of styles or allow our girls to do so, are we adhering to the Bible's admonition to be discreet and chaste?

To gain a deeper understanding of our responsibility to instill these precepts of discretion and chastity, it would behoove us to examine these concepts more fully. What do these two words actually embody? First, the word discreet is defined as "having a judicious reserve in speech and behavior, unpretentious, showing good judgment." The Greek word is **sophron** (pronounced *so'-frone*) and means "safe, sound in mind, self-controlled, to save, deliver, protect." From these definitions, we can conclude that discreet behavior will cause one to be wise in her speech and conduct. This self-controlled demeanor will be a protection for the mind and will save that person from getting involved in unwise situations. Good judgment will govern every aspect of life.

The other word we are taking into account is **chaste**, meaning "morally pure, modest, abstaining from unlawful sexual intercourse, not overdone in style." The Greek word used is **hagnos** (pronounced *hag-nos'*) and is defined as "clean, innocent, modest, perfect, pure."

Let us pause and consider some questions in the light of these two words. How many still retain their sense of innocence in this world today? Are we teaching our girls to be modest and self-controlled in their speech and behavior? Are they learning to walk, talk, dress, and act like ladies? What kind of entertainment do we allow to creep into our youth groups? Does purity still remain a standard of excellence we teach our children to attain unto? Do we allow our young people to engage in actions that could possibly compromise their morality?

How can we insure that the passage of purity remains intact for our posterity? Quite simply, by modeling it, instilling it, and enforcing it daily in our homes and churches. If the word **enforce** seems a bit strong to you, might I remind you that when laws are enforced, the end result is a safer society. Likewise, when ground rules are set in place and acted upon within our homes and churches, they will produce an atmosphere of safety. I am thankful for parents who established boundaries in my life. One time when I questioned my mother's strict guidelines, she lovingly told me she trusted me but didn't trust my flesh. Mom was a wise woman, and because of her continual loving constraint upon my life, the principles of morality and virtue were established in me and are still intact to this day.

In like manner, my earnest desire is to pass along the same pure precepts to my daughters. One creative way of doing this is to take our children shopping and to actively teach them how to buy modest clothing. For special occasions such as birthdays, I give my girls money so they can pick out their own presents. This serves to create a very profitable avenue whereby they can learn to make right clothing choices, and it also teaches them to become wise shoppers who can get the most for their money. What's more, it provides an opportunity to bond with them as we share a time of fun and relaxation at the mall. Through this method of constructive yet enjoyable instruction, long lasting principles of purity are being instilled.

Morever, it is extremely important to teach our young ladies to exercise discretion when interacting with the opposite sex. It seems to have become socially acceptable for girls to chase boys. Many times I have heard mothers complaining about forward girls phoning their sons and behaving in a bold, flirtatious manner. This sort of improper behavior can come about as a result of a lack of instruction concerning proper, ladylike behavior. To insure safe passage through the turbulent teen years and into adulthood, it would behoove us to instill principles of virtuous conduct within our children. Furthermore, our own interaction with the opposite sex should always be above reproach so as to set an example of excellence for others to attain unto.

In this out-of-control culture, we must actively take charge of our world by exercising our parental influence in a positive manner so as to preserve and protect our posterity from defilement. Even though our society is aggressively attacking morality and virtue as described in Isaiah 5:20:

> *"Woe unto them that call evil good, and good evil; that put darkness for light, and light for darkness; that put bitter for sweet, and sweet for bitter!"*

We do not have to sit idly by and watch it suck our children into its immoral morass. Isn't it time we become just as aggressive in our resistance to the evil infiltration of impurity? By teaching each succeeding generation to be discreet and chaste, the installation of principled purity will empower our offspring to excel in God's kingdom.

In order the show the importance of purchasing a certain product, a nationwide advertising campaign has coined this trademark question: "Got Milk?" Following in the same vein of thought concerning the magnitude of our buying into the purity principle, I would ask you, "Got discretion? Got chastity?" There is no better time than the present to reinstate the **passage of purity!**

Chapter Seven Footnote:

1. For further study on modesty, I have written a series of books entitled *Power Before the Throne*, *Reflecting the Glory*, and *Desired by the King*.

Housekeepers

OR HOMEBUILDERS

" . . . keepers at home, good, obedient to their own husbands,
that the word of God be not blasphemed."

*"A godly woman sure should be a Sarah to her lord, a Martha
to her company, a Mary to the Word."*   ~ *Charles Spurgeon*

The final portion of Paul's writings to women in Titus 2:3-5
encompasses three key areas: housekeeping, goodness, and
obedience. As this book comes to a close, I would like to examine each of these areas.

The first subject we will consider is that of being the keeper of the home. Houses come in all shapes, sizes, and styles;
however, there is one common element which brings warmth to
a home, that is, the lady of the manor. Mother Teresa said it so
well, "The woman is the heart of the home." There is an old
saying that is somewhat humorous yet conveys the magnitude
of the woman's influence upon her home and family. It simply
says, "If Mama ain't happy, ain't nobody happy!" Indeed, this
truism certainly encapsulates the ability a woman has to control
her environment for either good or bad. The way a lady inter-
acts with her family from sunrise to sunset can establish the
mood of the entire household. Chances are pretty good that if
Mama is cranky, everyone else will be out of sorts. Conversely,

if Mother is in a pleasant frame of mind, her peaceful attitude will flow soothingly through the life of her family. "Take from our souls the strain and stress, and let our ordered lives confess the beauty of Thy peace" (John Greenleaf Whittier). A housewife's job description encompasses so much more than cooking, cleaning, canning, or creating an inviting environment. Our daily actions will either build up or tear down our homes. God has entrusted us with the ability to joyfully brighten others' lives or to cast a dark shadow of gloom and doom. "Just as a little thread of gold, running through a fabric, brightens the whole garment, so women's work at home, while only the doing of little things, is like the golden gleam of sunlight that runs through and brightens all the fabric of civilization" (Laura Ingalls Wilder). What an incredible responsibility rests upon the shoulders of every wife and mother! "Life is too sweet to waste a day. It's up to you to make it sweet" (Sara Louise Delany).

Ordinary, mundane tasks can actually become avenues of extraordinary inspiration, and our prayer should always be, "Lord, use us, jars of clay that we are, to show forth Your all-surpassing power" (Verdell Davis). As the preceding thought-provoking chapters illustrate, the influence of every woman is so far-reaching on many differing levels. It is important to understand the lasting effect of our homes: "Home, a place that our feet may leave, but not our hearts." Why not take a moment to remember the many ways your mother's loving labor was a daily blessing in your life? Think about the many delicious meals she made, along with keeping a clean home and preparing an inviting ambience. Does the sound of her sacred, heartfelt prayers still echo through your subconscious? How thankful I am for my godly, praying mother and her dedication to God and her family! Truly, the potent effect of her joyful consecration lives on in many lives.

"When God's joy invades our lives, it spills over into everything we do and onto everyone we touch" (Charles Swindoll).

At one point when she was raising her five children, Mother was feeling bad because of her inability to be more involved in the different aspects of God's kingdom. However, Mom raised five children who all love God and are involved in His work in so many ways. Mother's spiritual influence has been compounded many times over through the ministries of her children and grandchildren. What a far-reaching, extraordinary impact her ordinary duties have had upon the work of the Lord! Don't ever underestimate the profound power which has been entrusted into your charge as a "keeper at home." "Ordinary work, which is what most of us do most of the time, is ordained by God every bit as much as is the extraordinary" (Elisabeth Elliot). Always remember that your ordinary efforts could extraordinarily affect eternal issues.

The next area of examination is that of being "good." In a world filled with many "bad" women, God's desire is for each of us to become a lady who is endowed with the quality of goodness. According to *Webster's Dictionary*, good is defined as "having positive or desirable qualities, suitable, serviceable, not spoiled, whole, sound, of high quality, discriminating, beneficial, competent, skilled, complete, thorough, safe, sure, valid, genuine, real, pleasant, enjoyable, favorable, virtuous, upright, benevolent, cheerful, loyal, staunch, well-behaved, obedient, socially correct, proper, to succeed, the valuable or useful part, goodness, merit." Wow, what a litany of lovely characteristics are embodied within this little four-letter word! Why not take a moment to contemplate every amazing aspect and attitude encapsulated in this coveted quality. While reflecting on each of these admirable character qualities, wouldn't it be beneficial to prayerfully consider how each of these goodly components can become an intrinsic part of your daily life?

"Grace was in all her steps, heaven in her eye, in every gesture dignity and love" (John Milton).

Continuing in our in-depth analysis of this scriptural passage, let us look at the injunction to be obedient to our husbands. The Greek word for obedient is **hupotasso** (pronounced *hoop-ot-as'-so*), meaning "to subordinate, to obey, be under obedience, put under, subdue, be in subjection to, submit self to." Paul used the exact same word in Ephesians 5:22 and Colossians 3:18 when addressing the topic of wifely submission.

Understandably, the subject of submitting has been the theme of several of my previous books, and to that end, I do not wish to be superfluous on this particular subject. However, I would like to share some interesting insights with you.

First, please allow me to say that submission is perhaps the most powerfully liberating and protective biblical concept found in the pages of Holy Writ. Contrary to what many may think, the one who submits is not in bondage but is actually put into a place of secure safety. When entering into a covenant of obedient submission with God, the woman is in fact placing herself under the Almighty's protection. Her obedience will then release His divine providence on her behalf. This truth has been so profoundly illustrated in my own life, and I would like to share a personal testimony concerning the power of this principle.

Several years ago I came under very heavy spiritual attack, and one incident in particular comes to mind. While I scrubbed my floor that afternoon, a hideous onslaught from the enemy was launched against me. Ferociously assaulting my spirit, satan taunted me about some awful circumstances taking place in my life. As the evil barrage escalated in intensity, diabolical ideas about cutting my hair were hurled against my tormented mind. Never in all my life had there ever been a struggle in this area of obedience. But at that moment, the urge to put a scissors to my uncut hair almost overpowered me. As the battle raged back and forth within my mind, a firm resolve to remain obedient to God's precepts started permeating my soul. Exerting both physical and spiritual effort, I began to withstand this horrible invasion of hell. Finally, after a time of intense struggle, the devil departed and the victory was won. Not until a much later date would I realize the magnitude of what had transpired in the spiritual realm on that fateful day.

Approximately four years after the above-mentioned incident, I wrote my initial book, entitled *Power Before the Throne*. At that point, the Lord gave me a much greater understanding concerning the power of submission in connection with a woman's uncut hair. As I wrote the book, an unexpected inheritance came my way from a distant aunt, which provided the means to pay for the entire first printing of my inaugural written work. I was totally amazed when it became necessary to reprint this book after its being on the market for only six weeks! As time went on, God continued to bless my writing ministry, which blossomed dramatically with numerous adult and children's books being written in the following months. Still I did not fully understand the miracle that was in the making.

Meanwhile, some very tragic events transpired in my life, and I found myself facing the trauma of divorce and single parenthood. Unbeknownst to me, my ex-husband had already started down a pathway of disobedience when I was confronted with that oppressive attack years earlier. After taking him captive, the enemy wanted to destroy me and my girls as well. Thankfully, the power of obedient submission became a shield of protection when the enemy came in like a flood, and in the days to come, God raised up a standard on our behalf. Abandoned by my former spouse, I felt the frightening misfortune of my circumstances threaten to overwhelm me. Nevertheless, my precious Lord and Master had gone before me and prepared a way of provision so we could survive those horrifically dark and lonely times. Through the writing and speaking ministry God had established in my life, He faithfully provided for all our needs. We have never lacked for anything, because He always takes care of His people. Just imagine for a moment if I had given in to the onslaught of satan and his hideous suggestion that I remove the protective covering of my uncut hair . . . *Power Before the Throne* and all the successive materials probably would have never been forthcoming, nor would my speaking ministry have been birthed. The outcome of my situation would have been far more tragic because I would have thwarted God's plan of providence through my disobedience.

David declared in Psalm 37:25:

> *"I have been young, and now am old; yet have I not seen the righteous forsaken, nor his seed begging bread."*

I learned firsthand how relevant and reliable God's promises are to those who keep His covenant. When the enemy's aggression was so cruelly launched against me and my daughters, the power of obedient submission became our means of salvation. In His amazing foresight, the Lord understood the vulnerability of the woman, so He set in place a means of protection and provision if she will submit to His Word and ways. If your earthly spouse forsakes you, there is a heavenly Husband who will never leave nor forsake you. Isaiah 54:5 avers:

"For thy Maker is thine husband; the LORD of hosts is his name; and thy Redeemer the Holy One of Israel; The God of the whole earth shall he be called."

Through the mastery of submission, we can walk in complete confidence of the validity and authority of God's Word. He always shows mercy to those who love Him and keep His commandments.[1] Oh, the power and promise of obedience!

At the conclusion of this particular passage of Scripture, the apostle Paul identified the underlying impetus for our adherence to these biblical principles, "that the word of God be not blasphemed." Blaspheme is defined as "to speak of God or something sacred in an irreverent or forbidden manner, to reproach." Our failure to obey God's laws can actually bring a reproach against God's kingdom and His Word. On the other hand, if we faithfully fulfill His sacred commandments, our becoming behavior will be a marvelous testimony to the world. Through our actions, God's Word can suffer an ugly reproach or be beautifully enhanced. The ability to make the gospel look good or bad lies within the grasp of every woman.

As we endeavor to build up our homes, let us always strive to be gracious, beautiful women from the inside out. "Some people, no matter how old they get, never lose their beauty—they merely move it from their faces into their hearts" (Anonymous). May we continually do all in our power to "**be in behaviour as becometh holiness!**"

Chapter Eight Footnote:

1. Exodus 20:6; Deuteronomy 5:10.

REFERENCE BIBLIOGRAPHY

Almighty God. *The Holy Bible.*

Andrews, Andy. *The Lost Choice.* Nelson Books, Nashville, TN.

Countryman, J., editor and compiler. *God's Promises to Mothers.* A division of Thomas Nelson, Inc.

Feldhahn, Shaunti. *For Women Only—What You Need to Know About the Inner Lives of Men.* Multnomah Publishers, Sisters, OR.

Fischer-Mirkin, Toby. *Dress Code—Understanding the Hidden Meanings of Women's Clothes.* Clarkson Potter/Publishers, New York, NY.

Freeman, Dr. Criswell. *Love Is. . . .* Delaney Street Press.

Harley, Willard F., Jr. *His Needs, Her Needs—Building an Affair Proof Marriage.* Baker House Books, Grand Rapids, MI.

Knight, Walter B. *Knight's Master Book of New Illustrations.* Wm. B. Eerdmans Publishing Company, Grand Rapids, MI.

P.C. Study Bible 3.1. Reference Library.

Rosberg, Dr. Gary and Barbara. *40 Unforgettable Dates with Your Mate—Creative Ways to Meet the Love Needs of Husbands and Wives.* Tyndale House Publishers, Wheaton, IL.

Schlessinger, Dr. Laura. *The Proper Care and Feeding of Husbands.* Harper Collins Publishers, New York, NY.

Smith, Debra White. *Romancing Your Husband—Enjoying a Passionate Life Together*. Harvest House Publishers, Eugene, OR.

Strong, James, S.T.D., LL.D. *Abingdon's Strong's Exhaustive Concordance of the Bible*. Abingdon, Nashville, TN.

Telushkin, Rabbi Joseph. *The Book of Jewish Values– A Day- by- Day Guide to Ethical Living*. Bell Tower, New York, NY.

Thomas, Gary. *Sacred Marriage*. Zondervan, Grand Rapids, MI.

Webster's New Reference Library. A Nelson/Regency Publication, Thomas Nelson Publishers, Nashville–Camden–New York.

ABOUT THE AUTHOR

Ruth Harvey is the wife of Rev. Steven Harvey and mother of two daughters, Angelica and Miriam. Currently residing in Connecticut, Harvey is also the national Daughters of Zion Director, an international speaker, and recording artist. She is the author of several best-selling books, including the well-loved book, *Power Before the Throne*. Ruth's skillful writing, anointed speaking, and dynamic singing pulsate with her intense passion for God, His Kingdom, the Word, and prayer.

Harvey began her writing career in 1998 at the earnest request of many people who desired that her teaching insights be put into written form. While writing her first book, *Power Before the Throne*, she received an unexpected inheritance from a distant aunt which provided the financial means to pay for the entire printing of her inaugural work. In six short weeks, the first printing of this book almost completely sold out, necessitating ongoing reprints. Because of the overnight success of her first

book, Harvey has gone on to write several more titles, including an entire children's series. People from around the world have been positively impacted through her inspirational writing, speaking, and singing ministry. All of Harvey's products are available for purchase on her web site, www.positivepowerofholiness.com.

OTHER PRODUCTS

by Ruth Harvey (formerly Ruth Rieder):

Books:
Power Before the Throne
Reflecting the Glory
Covenant by Sacrifice
Desired by the King
Relic or Relevant
Beauty or The Beast

Books for children (Kingdom Kids series):
Angels Watching Over Me
Kingdom Clothing
Marble Palaces or Painted Barns
God's Jewels
Adorned for the King
The Enclosed Garden

The Positive Power of Holiness:
Interactive Study Guide
Student Test Pack
Teacher Test Pack
Video (90 minutes)
Cassette (90 minutes)

Keys to Knowing God cassettes:
Prayer
Biblical Fasting
Building Prayer Equity
Knowing God Through His Word
The Power of Discipline

Music (CD and cassette):
Power in Praisin'

To order by mail, use form on next page.

Send order form with check or money order to:
Ruth Harvey
3 Lois Lane
Enfield, CT 06082

Shipping address:
Name: _____
Address:_____
City, State, Zip: _____
Telephone (optional): _____
E-mail (optional): _____

Product	Price	Quantity	Subtotal
Becoming Behavior	12.00		
Power Before the Throne	9.00		
Reflecting the Glory	10.00		
Covenant by Sacrifice	11.00		
Desired by the King	11.00		
Relic or Relevant	12.95		
Beauty or the Beast	11.00		
Angels Watching Over Me	6.00		
Kingdom Clothing	6.00		
Marble Palaces or Painted Barns	6.00		
God's Jewels	6.00		
Adorned for the King	6.00		
The Enclosed Garden	6.00		
Holiness: Interactive Study Guide	12.00		
Holiness: Student Test Pack	8.00		
Holiness: Teacher Test Pack	8.00		
Holiness: Video	27.00		
Holiness: Cassette	11.00		
Prayer	9.00		
Biblical Fasting	9.00		
Building Prayer Equity	9.00		
Knowing God Through His Word	9.00		
The Power of Discipline	9.00		
Power in Praisin' (CD)	18.00		
Power in Praisin' (cassette)	11.00		
(Shipping is included in prices)	**Total:**		